CONTENTS

GRADE 7

UNIT 1 ▪ GRAMMAR

Sentences

Kinds of Sentences 1
Complete Subjects and Complete Predicates 2
Simple Subjects and Simple Predicates 3
Compound Subjects and Compound Predicates 4
Compound Sentences 5
Correcting Fragments and Run-on Sentences 6
Mechanics: Punctuating Sentences 7
Vocabulary Building: Using Context Clues 8
Grammar and Writing Connection: Combining Sentences 9

UNIT 2 ▪ WRITING

Writing Personal Narratives

Group Writing: A Personal Narrative 10
Thinking and Writing: General and Specific 11
Proofreading: Step 4 12

UNIT 3 ▪ GRAMMAR

Nouns

Kinds of Nouns 13
Singular and Plural Nouns 14
Possessive Nouns 15
Collective and Compound Nouns 16
Appositives 17
Mechanics: Forming Possessive Nouns and Contractions 18
Mechanics: Capitalizing Proper Nouns 19
Vocabulary Building: How Language Changes 20
Grammar and Writing Connection: Combining Sentences 21

UNIT 4 ▪ WRITING

Writing Short Stories

Group Writing: A Short Story 22
Thinking and Writing: Understanding Point of View 23
Proofreading: Step 4 24

UNIT 5 ▪ GRAMMAR

Verbs

Action Verbs 25
Verbs with Direct Objects 26
Verbs with Indirect Objects 27
Linking Verbs 28
Present, Past, and Future Tenses 29
Verb Phrases 30
Present and Past Progressive Forms 31
Perfect Tenses 32
Irregular Verbs I 33
Irregular Verbs II 34
Subject-Verb Agreement 35
Mechanics: Using Commas to Separate Parts of a Sentence 36
Vocabulary Building: Word Choice 37
Grammar and Writing Connection: Using Active and Passive Voices 38

UNIT 6 ▪ WRITING

Writing Explanations

Group Writing: An Explanatory Paragraph 39
Thinking and Writing: Comparing and Contrasting 40
Proofreading: Step 4 41

UNIT 7 ▪ GRAMMAR

Pronouns

Personal Pronouns 42
Pronouns and Antecedents 43
Using Pronouns Correctly 44
Possessive Pronouns 45
Indefinite Pronouns 46
Subject-Verb Agreement with Indefinite Pronouns 47
Reflexive and Intensive Pronouns 48
Interrogative and Demonstrative Pronouns 49
Mechanics: Using Abbreviations 50
Vocabulary Building: Homophones and Homographs 51
Grammar and Writing Connection: Combining Sentences 52

UNIT 8 ▪ WRITING

Writing Biographical Sketches

Group Writing: A Biographical Sketch 53
Thinking and Writing: Understanding Sequence 54
Proofreading: Step 4 55

UNIT 9 ▪ GRAMMAR

Adjectives and Adverbs

Adjectives 56
Articles and Proper Adjectives 57
Comparative and Superlative Adjectives I 58
Comparative and Superlative Adjectives II 59
Demonstrative Adjectives 60
Adverbs 61
Comparative and Superlative Adverbs 62
Avoiding Double Negatives 63
Using Adjectives and Adverbs 64
Mechanics: Commas with Dates, Addresses, and Names 65
Vocabulary Building: Synonyms and Antonyms 66
Grammar and Writing Connection: Combining Sentences 67

UNIT 10 ▪ WRITING

Writing Descriptions

Group Writing: A Description 68
Thinking and Writing: Classifying 69
Proofreading: Step 4 70

UNIT 11 ▪ GRAMMAR

Prepositions, Conjunctions, and Interjections

Prepositions and Prepositional Phrases 71
Using Pronouns in Prepositional Phrases 72
Prepositional Phrases as Adjectives or Adverbs 73
Using Verbs After Prepositional Phrases 74
Conjunctions 75
Making Verbs Agree with Compound Subjects 76
Interjections 77
Mechanics: Using Semicolons and Colons 78
Vocabulary Building: Prefixes 79
Grammar and Writing Connection: Combining Sentences 80

UNIT 12 ▪ WRITING

Writing Editorials

Group Writing: An Editorial 81
Thinking and Writing: Faulty Methods of Persuasion 82
Proofreading: Step 4 83

UNIT 13 ▪ GRAMMAR

Complex Sentences and Verbals

Sentences and Clauses 84
Complex Sentences 85
Adjective Clauses 86
Adverb Clauses 87
Participles and Participial Phrases 88
Gerunds 89
Infinitives 90
Mechanics: Using Commas with Clauses 91
Vocabulary Building: Suffixes 92
Grammar and Writing Connection: Parallel Structure 93

UNIT 14 ▪ WRITING

Writing Research Reports

Group Writing: A Research Report 94
Thinking and Writing: Understanding Cause and Effect 95
Proofreading: Step 4 96

Answers T1–T48

Name ____________________

Kinds of Sentences

A **sentence** is a group of words that expresses a complete thought.
Every sentence begins with a capital letter and ends with a punctuation mark.

A **declarative sentence** makes a statement and ends with a period.

Marco Polo was born in 1254.

An **interrogative sentence** asks a question and ends with a question mark.

Did you know that he was the most famous European traveler in the Far East?

An **imperative sentence** commands or requests and ends with a period.

Read his biography.

An **exclamatory sentence** expresses strong feeling and ends with an exclamation mark.

He had some extraordinary adventures!

A. Write whether each sentence is **declarative**, **interrogative**, **exclamatory**, or **imperative**.

1. Have you heard of Marco Polo? ____________

2. In 1271, he was a boy in Venice, Italy. ____________

3. Read how he began an amazing journey. ____________

4. He, his father, and his uncle set out for China. ____________

5. What a journey it was! ____________

B. Use the correct capitalization and punctuation marks for each sentence. Then write whether it is **declarative**, **interrogative**, **exclamatory**, or **imperative**.

6. their adventure lasted twenty-four years ____________

7. they traveled by ship, by camel, and on foot ____________

8. what amazing things they did ____________

9. read about their wonderful experiences ____________

10. do you know about the Emperor Kublai Khan ____________

11. marco became an advisor to the emperor ____________

12. the Polos traveled throughout China and to Japan ____________

13. trace his route on a map ____________

Extension: Have students write four examples for each of the four kinds of sentences. Then have students exchange papers and punctuate each others sentences.

PRACTICE-2

Name

Complete Subjects and Complete Predicates

The **complete subject** of a sentence includes all the words that tell whom or what the sentence is about.
The **complete predicate** of a sentence includes all the words that tell what the subject does or is.

Complete Subject	**Complete Predicate**
That girl with the red hair	belongs to the whitewater rafting club.

Underline the complete subject once and the complete predicate twice. Write *(You)* to identify the complete subject of an imperative sentence.

1. Our whitewater rafting club took a raft trip last week.
2. Many people in this area enjoy whitewater rafting.
3. Adventurous rafters ride down quiet rivers and dangerous rapids.
4. Have you ever tried riding down a river in a raft?
5. Several parents drove our rafts and gear to the river.
6. We launched our raft into the Farmington River early in the morning.
7. There were five of us aboard the raft.
8. Find Ben in this picture from the trip.
9. The brightly colored raft rushed down the rapids.
10. Our group paddled to the shore for a rest at around ten A. M.
11. There were dozens of whitewater rafters out on the river that day.
12. Past rocks and boulders raced the boats.
13. Can you imagine the excitement of the trip?
14. Rapids made parts of the trip very exciting.
15. We ran through one very tricky set of rocky rapids.
16. The raft nearly capsized several times.
17. We quickly adopted whitewater rafting as our favorite sport.
18. All five of us want another trip very soon.
19. There is an especially difficult trip next June.

Extension: Have students write five sentences about a favorite sport or hobby. Have them exchange papers with a partner who will underline the complete subject once and the complete predicate twice.

Name

Simple Subjects and Simple Predicates

The **simple subject** is the main word or words in the complete subject.
The **simple predicate** is the main word or words in the complete predicate.

Complete Subject — **Complete Predicate**

The **airplanes** of the early 1900s **flew** only short distances.

↑ **Simple Subject** ↑ **Simple Predicate**

Underline the simple subject of each sentence once and the simple predicate twice.

1. There was a famous prize for flyers during the early 1900s.
2. The prize awarded $25,000 for the first solo airplane flight across the Atlantic Ocean.
3. Many aviators died in pursuit of this famous Ortieg prize.
4. An unknown American flyer tried for the prize in 1927.
5. People in St. Louis gave Charles Lindbergh money for a plane.
6. Lindbergh named his plane *The Spirit of St. Louis.*
7. Lindbergh's small plane left from Roosevelt Field, an airfield on Long Island, on May 20, 1927.
8. Lindbergh's plane stayed in the air for almost a day and a half.
9. The pilot endured many hardships during the flight.
10. Temperatures inside the plane were very cold.
11. Exhaustion threatened him throughout the flight.
12. Can you imagine Lindbergh's feelings during the flight?
13. *The Spirit of St. Louis* landed in Paris, France, on May 21, 1927.
14. There were thousands of people at the airport.
15. The tall American completed the first solo flight across the Atlantic.
16. He covered more than 3,600 miles in 33 hours.
17. Here is a picture of Lindbergh's plane on its arrival at the airfield near Paris.
18. People around the world honored Lindbergh for his accomplishment.
19. His admirers gave him the nickname "The Lone Eagle."
20. We read about the flight in Lindbergh's autobiography.

Extension: Have students copy five sentences from a newspaper or magazine and then underline the simple subject and simple predicate in each.

Name

Compound Subjects and Compound Predicates

A **compound subject** is two or more simple subjects with the same predicate.

Mark and Linda packed for a day at the beach.

A **compound predicate** is two or more simple predicates with the same subject.

The two friends stopped and ate their picnic lunch.

A **coordinating conjunction**, or connecting word, such as *and, or,* or *but* connects the parts of a compound subject or predicate.

Write whether each sentence contains a **compound subject** or a **compound predicate**. Then write the simple subjects or simple predicates in each compound.

1. Mark and Linda have planned a trip to Baker Park.

2. They organized their things and packed their knapsacks.

3. At nine o'clock they went down Sprain Street and waited for a bus.

4. The driver and the other passengers smiled at the sight of them.

5. Each of them had enough gear for a week and wobbled under the weight.

6. A man in a business suit and a young woman in running clothes helped the two into seats.

7. The bus quickly pulled into traffic and was on its way.

8. Mark and his friend arrived at the park by ten o'clock.

9. They hurriedly made their way to the beach area and spread their blankets.

Extension: Have students write four original sentences containing a simple subject and a simple predicate. Then have students exchange papers, adding words so that the simple subject or simple predicate becomes compound.

PRACTICE-5

Name

Compound Sentences

A **simple sentence** has one complete subject and one complete predicate.
A **compound sentence** contains two or more simple sentences joined by a comma and a conjunction or by a semicolon.

Simple Sentence

Thousands of people visit Grand Canyon National Park every year;
they enjoy everything from hikes to rides down the Colorado River.

Simple Sentence

Write whether each sentence is a **simple** sentence or a **compound** sentence.

1. Last summer, our family took a trip to the Southwest. __________
2. We hiked down the canyon, and we saw its beauty firsthand. __________
3. We also drove around the canyon's rim to see the spectacular views. __________
4. We spent three days at the Grand Canyon; then we went on to see the Painted Desert. __________
5. We had never seen anything quite like the colors of the Painted Desert. __________
6. We enjoyed seeing these landmarks, but the biggest thrill came later. __________
7. The family spent a week at the Mesquite Ranch. __________
8. We helped the cowhands with the ranch's cattle, or we cared for the many horses on the ranch. __________
9. After chores, we went to the corral for our horses, or we went down to the lake for a nice cool swim. __________
10. We went waterskiing, and we even rode behind the speedboat on a long, plastic "torpedo." __________
11. Several times, we hiked to a trout stream. __________
12. For three days we went on a cattle drive; we lived like the cowhands of the Old West. __________

Extension: Have students write five simple sentences. Then have students exchange papers and add words so that the sentences become compound.

PRACTICE-6

Name ______________________________

Correcting Fragments and Run-on Sentences

A **sentence fragment** is a group of words that is only part of a sentence. It does not have both a subject and a predicate, and it does not express a complete thought.

No Predicate Part: Hundreds of daring adventurers.
No Subject Part: Traveling to the South Pole.

A **run-on sentence** is two or more sentences run together without correct punctuation.

Sentence | **Sentence**
Antarctic weather is fierce many met disastrous fates.

A. Write whether each item is a **fragment** or a **run-on**.

1. ______________ One of the greatest journeys of all time was that of Captain Robert F. Scott it ended in tragic failure.

2. ______________ Scott's party of men and sledges (heavy wooden sleds).

3. ______________ At about the same time, a group of Norwegian explorers also set out for the pole they were led by Roald Amundsen.

4. ______________ Scott's group, ill-prepared and burdened by the heavy, unsuitable equipment.

5. ______________ Upon his arrival at the South Pole, Scott found Amundsen's flag and markers the Norwegians had beat the British by five weeks.

B. Correct each of the fragments and run-ons from Part A. Write the correct sentences below.

6. ______________________________

____

7. ______________________________

____

8. ______________________________

____

9. ______________________________

____

10. ______________________________

____

Extension: Have students write two sentence fragments and two run-on sentences. Then have students exchange papers and rewrite each item correctly.

Name

Mechanics: Punctuating Sentences

Use a **period** to end a declarative or an imperative sentence.

A paddle boat is a boat propelled by a paddle wheel.

Use a **question mark** to end an interrogative sentence.

Did you know that the paddle wheel can be at the side or the rear of the boat?

Use an **exclamation mark** to end an exclamatory sentence.

That boat is exciting to watch!

Use a **comma** before the conjunction in a compound sentence, or join the parts with a **semicolon**.

The *Clermont* was a paddle boat, and its side paddle was powered by steam engines.
The *Clermont* was a paddle boat; its side paddle was powered by steam engines.

Add the correct punctuation mark at the end of each sentence.

1. Have you ever been on an old-fashioned boat
2. Last week, the school's history club boarded the *River Star*
3. Here is a model of the boat
4. Be careful
5. What a fantastic boat it is
6. Look at these pictures of the club on the dock
7. Can you see Miguel and Allyson up on the captain's bridge
8. Please, handle the pictures carefully
9. We boarded the boat as quickly as possible
10. The boat soon filled with many other passengers as well
11. Was that roar the engines starting up
12. We watched the giant paddle wheel at the back of the boat
13. People call this kind of boat a sternwheeler
14. Side-wheelers have paddle wheels on the sides
15. Don't interrupt
16. We traveled almost thirty miles up the river
17. Captain Clark even let some of us onto the captain's bridge
18. Several students took a turn at the giant steering wheel
19. What a thrill it was
20. We felt like real Mississippi River pilots

Extension: Have students copy five sentences from a science or history text, omitting punctuation. Then have them exchange papers and punctuate each other's sentences.

Name ______________________________

Vocabulary Building: Using Context Clues

You can sometimes figure out the meaning of an unfamiliar word by looking at its **context**, or the words that come before or after it.

When we were tourists in Greece, we went on many excursions to see the sights.

The words *tourists* and *see the sights* give you a clue to the definition of *excursions*, which means, "short trips made especially for pleasure, or for a specific purpose."

Write the meaning of each underlined word. Use context clues to help you. Then, use a dictionary to check your work.

1. The Greek guide led us past the seats and onto the stage of the giant, outdoor amphitheater.

____

2. On the stage, eloquent actors had recited the stirring lines of many ancient dramas.

____

3. The downfall of most tragic heroes came about because of their hubris, or exaggerated pride.

____

4. We directed our queries about the place to our guide, who answered all our questions.

____

5. We planned to return to the stage on subsequent visits.

____

6. Long ago, theater-goers walked along the elegant promenade outside the arena.

____

7. Theater-goers often ate lavish dinners of expensive and perfectly prepared food.

____

8. Audiences at the dramas were quiet, never raucous or disruptive.

____

9. In a nearby gift shop, we searched for a memento of our visit.

____

Extension: Invite students to find words in the dictionary that they think their classmates will not know. Have them write sentences with context clues for those words. Exchanging papers, students can see how well they did with their clues by how closely the other students came to defining the words.

PRACTICE-9

Name

Grammar and Writing Connection: Combining Sentences

When you write, you often need to tell when events happened or why. Sometimes you can combine sentences to show a relationship of events.
You can use the connecting words *after, before, since, until, when,* and *while* to show a relationship of events in time.

Separate: I was very excited. The tennis lesson began.
Combined: I was very excited when the tennis lesson began.

You can use the connecting words *because, if, so that,* or *since* to show a relationship of reason or condition.

Separate: My family was at the lesson. I wanted to do well.
Combined: Because my family was at the lesson, I wanted to do well.

Use a comma at the end of the clause when the connecting word begins a sentence. A comma is not used when the connecting word and clause come at the end of the new sentence.

Combine each pair of sentences. Use the connecting words listed above.

1. I rushed to the tennis center. School ended at three o'clock.

___

2. I ran as hard as I could. I didn't want to be late.

___

3. I arrived. I got ready as quickly as I could.

___

4. It was my first lesson. My instructor went very slowly.

___

5. I learned to hold the racquet. I learned to hit the ball.

___

6. We hit the ball back and forth. I got better and better at it.

___

Extension: Have students write two pairs of short separate sentences that can be combined to show a relationship of ideas and a relationship of reason. Then have students exchange papers and combine the sentences.

PRACTICE-10

Name

Group Writing: A Personal Narrative

A **personal narrative** is a true story based on your own experience. An effective personal narrative has a **beginning sentence** that captures the reader's attention and states the main idea of the story. **Details** are a list of events that support the narrative's main idea and are given in **chronological order**. **Transition words** or phrases used in the narrative help clarify how details are related in time. The **last sentence** ties up the events and leaves the reader with something to think about.

Read this first paragraph from a personal narrative. Then answer the questions that follow.

This summer, I learned just how hard clowning around can be. In July, my family went to Baraboo, Wisconsin. That is the home of a circus museum and a school for clowns. There, I put on grease paint, an outlandish costume, and, for a day, I tried to be a *real* clown. Professional clowns showed me some tricks. I learned how twenty clowns can come out of a car. I practiced with the trained bears. I learned how to trip over my big shoes and fall on my face. Finally, I performed under a genuine "big top" in front of an audience.

1. What is the main idea of this narrative?

2. What details in this paragraph support the main idea?

3. For whom do you think the writer created this narrative?

4. What would you like to learn more about?

5. How would you end this narrative? Write a closing sentence.

Extension: Have students continue the narrative about the school for clowns and the performance referred to in the paragraph on this page.

Name ____

Thinking and Writing: General and Specific

General terms refer to many different things or activities. **Specific terms** refer to particular things or activities within a general category.

General	Specific	More Specific
plant	flower	tulip

Ideas, like things and activities, can also be general or specific.

A. Write three specific details beneath each general statement.

1. On Saturday, Gina, Karen, and Meg went to the amusement park.

____

____

____

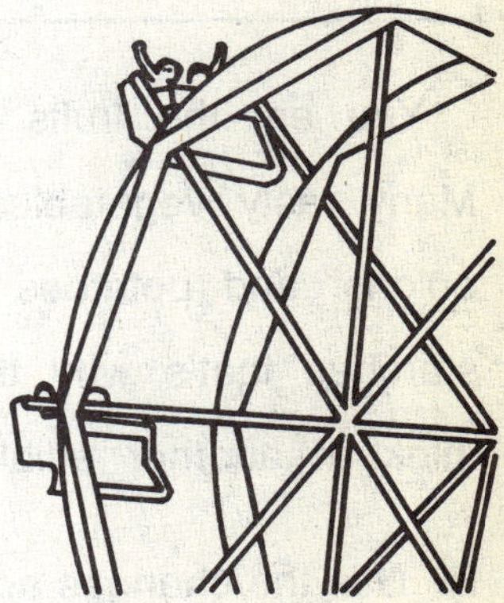

2. Bugsy the Clown performs at the amusement park.

____

____

____

B. Write a general statement covering each set of details about Gina, Karen, and Meg's trip to the amusement park.

3. ____

The girls climbed into the car.
The car raced up and down the roller coaster track.
The people in the cars screamed with pleasure at each dip.

4. ____

Each contestant struck a large piece of metal with a big hammer.
Meg tried the contest first.
Gina swung the hammer and hit the bell.

5. ____

A trained seal did tricks with a giant beach ball.
Donnie the Wonder Dog did wonderful stunts.
A lion tamer's lions jumped through a hoop.

Extension: Have students work with a partner to develop a list of specific terms for these general terms: *plant, animal, mineral, sport.*

Name

Proofreading: Step 4

Indent	¶
Add	∧
Add a comma	∧,
Add quotation marks	∨ ∨
Add a period	⊙
Take out	ℓ
Capitalize	≡
Make a small letter	/
Reverse the order	∽

Read the following paragraph about some edible parts of plants. Check to see if there are any sentence fragments. Then, see if all the sentences have correct end punctuation. Also, see if compound sentences are punctuated correctly.

A. Use the proofreading marks to make any changes or corrections in the paragraph.

You eat the fruits of many plants and you also eat the roots and stems Many tasty vegetables are roots and stems. Think of a few examples Carrots, onions, and potatoes are all edible roots Are storage places for sugars and starches that's why they often taste sweet? Celery is an edible stem, can you think of another edible stem! What a varied menu nature presents to us

B. Use the changes and corrections you marked above to write the paragraph correctly on the lines below.

Name ______________________________

Kinds of Nouns

A **noun** is a word that names a person, place, thing, or idea.
A **concrete noun** names something that can be seen or touched. An **abstract noun** names something that cannot be seen or touched.

Concrete Nouns: girl, town, lake, book
Abstract Nouns: philosophy, social studies, curiosity, intelligence

A **common noun** names a nonspecific, or general, person, place, thing, or idea. A **proper noun** names a specific person, place, thing, or idea.

Common Nouns: brother, friend, city, state, book
Proper Nouns: Charlie, Phyllis, Tulsa, California, *The Call of the Wild*

A. Above the underlined nouns, write **C** if it is a concrete noun or **A** if it is abstract.

1. Tina writes stories about many different things.

2. The ideas come to Tina from her experiences and her feelings.

3. Like Sarah, Tina gets new ideas all the time.

4. Each night Tina puts a story in her notebook.

5. She bought the book at Lawford's Stationery Store downtown.

B. Underline the common nouns in each sentence once and the proper nouns twice.

6. Mrs. Childs recommended this particular volume to her.

7. Some stories are only a few lines long.

8. Her favorite tale is about a young girl from colonial Virginia.

9. The story is about her adventures in the American Revolution.

10. At the end, the girl helps General Washington at the Battle of Yorktown.

11. Barbara wrote the story for a contest at her school.

12. People entered stories in several different categories.

13. Barbara won a prize.

14. She was thrilled with the books she won—and with the cash.

15. She published several stories in her newspaper last year.

16. This year she works for the paper and magazine at her school.

Extension: Have students make two columns on a piece of paper and label those columns *Concrete Nouns* and *Abstract Nouns*. Then have students see how many nouns they can enter in each column in five minutes.

Name

Singular and Plural Nouns

A **singular noun** names one person, place, or thing. A **plural noun** names more than one person, place, or thing. To form the plural of most nouns, add *s* at the end of the word. Follow these rules for spelling other plural nouns:

- Add *es* to nouns ending with *s, ss, x, zz, ch,* and *sh*, like *arch-arches.*
- Change *y* to *i* and add *es* to nouns ending with a consonant and *y*, like *story-stories.*
- Add *s* to nouns ending with a vowel and *y*, like *boy-boys*.
- Add *s* to nouns ending with a vowel and *o*, like *radio-radios.*
- Usually add *s* to nouns ending with a consonant and *o*, like *piano-pianos*, but sometimes add *es*, like *veto-vetoes*.
- Add *s* to all nouns ending in *ff*, and some ending in *f* or *fe*, like *roof-roofs* or *safe-safes*.
- Change *f* to *v* and add *es* for many nouns ending in *lf*, like *half-halves,* and some ending in *f* or *fe*, like *life-lives*.
- Change the spelling of some irregular nouns, like *foot-feet*.
- Keep the same spelling for some irregular nouns, like *deer-deer*.

A. Underline the plural nouns in these sentences.

1. Dana and Lina are taking art classes this year.
2. The girls have an hour-long class each Tuesday and Thursday.
3. Each class has several periods.
4. The students can study drawing, painting, or sculpting.
5. Dana particularly enjoys her drawing sessions.
6. She works with boxes of chalk as well as pen and ink.
7. This week she is making pictures of cows, sheep, horses, and cattle.
8. She is making illustrations for a report on agriculture.
9. Some children in the class illustrate stories.
10. They insert pictures into their favorite tales and novels.

B. Complete each sentence by writing the correct plural form of the word in parentheses.

11. Other young ________________ enjoy oil painting. (artist)
12. They use ________________ and palette ________________ for their works. (brush, knife)
13. Lina has finished so many ________________ that she will have an exhibit. (drawing)
14. "It feels just like singing ________________ in a concert," she says. (solo)
15. Her father is making ________________ of the exhibit. (video)

Extension: Have students rewrite the underlined nouns in Part A, making each plural noun singular.

PRACTICE-15

Name ______________________________

Possessive Nouns

____

A **possessive noun** names who or what has something.
Use an **apostrophe** and **s ('s)** to form the possessive of most singular nouns and of plural nouns that do not end with *s*.

Janice → Janice's   car → car's   children → children's

Use only an apostrophe **(')** to form the possessive of plural nouns that end with *s*.

dogs → dogs'   babies → babies'   Lopezes → Lopezes'

A. Underline the possessive noun(s) in each sentence.

1. *Charlotte's Web* is one of the most famous books of all time.
2. In fact, it is many people's favorite children's book.
3. The book's author is E. B. White, a well-known American author.
4. White's reputation was first made with essays.
5. Mount Vernon, New York, was the author's birthplace.
6. By the time he was twenty-five years old, he was contributing essays to *The New Yorker*, the country's leading literary magazine.
7. The informal, witty style of White's essays won the writer a large and loyal following of readers.
8. In 1945, he surprised many people with his first young people's book, *Stuart Little*.
9. Seven years later, *Charlotte's Web* appeared, and it quickly became a young reader's classic.
10. White's only other children's book, *The Trumpet of the Swan*, tells of a young swan's inability to make a swan's trumpeting sound.

B. Complete each sentence with the correct possessive form of the noun in parentheses.

11. White spent much of his adult life in ____________________ woodlands. (Maine)
12. The whole ____________________ appreciation for his works was expressed in many ways. (country)
13. In 1963, White was awarded the ____________________ special Medal of Freedom. (President)
14. Later, in 1978, he won one of the professional ____________________ highest distinctions, a special Pulitzer Prize citation. (writer)
15. Most of all, his works are treasured in ____________________ memories. (people)

Extension: Have students write four sentences for each of these words: *writer, author, library,* and *book.* Have them use the plural possessive form in two of the sentences and the singular possessive form in the other two.

Name ______________________________

Collective and Compound Nouns

A **collective noun** names a group of people or things. *Family, class, team,* and *bunch* are collective nouns.
When the collective noun refers to a group as a whole, use the singular form of a verb after it.

The drama class goes on a trip to the theater every Thursday.

When the collective noun refers to the individual members of a group, use the plural form of a verb.

The drama class applaud their favorite performers.

A **compound noun** is made up of two or more words that act as a single noun. Form the plural of compound nouns by changing the most important word in the compound.

sister-in-law → sisters-in-law   living room → living rooms

A. Underline each collective noun once and each compound noun twice.

1. The campground fills up with people very quickly at this time of year.
2. One group comes from Chicago every year at this time.
3. The staff of the campground always enjoys the summer holidays.
4. The social director organizes games, contests, and other events for the people.
5. Sing-alongs are fun for many campers.
6. Nora's brother-in-law puts together a story-telling contest each year.
7. Every camp member makes up a special story for the contest.
8. The audience picks the winner of the "Best Story of the Night" award.
9. Jamie's quartet sings in the contest every time.
10. Our junior high class wants to take a trip to the campground as well.

B. Circle **S** if the underlined word is singular or **P** if it is plural.

11. The campfires did not shed enough light. P S
12. Each person brought their own flashlight. P S
13. We thought we heard mountain lions. P S
14. Our group was not frightened by the noise. P S
15. We would like to go camping again in a few weekends. P S

Extension: Have students write two sentences for each of these collective nouns: *group, team, class.* Have them give the collective noun a singular meaning in the first sentence and a plural meaning in the second sentence.

Name

Appositives

An **appositive** is a word or group of words that immediately follows a noun and identifies or explains it.

Appositive

My sister, a girl of sixteen, has written stories for many years.

Use commas to set off most appositives from the rest of the sentence.

A. Underline the appositive in each sentence. Then draw two lines under the noun the appositive identifies.

1. Gerri, my older sister, writes wonderful stories.

2. Last week, she created a wonderful story, "The Weavers of Glen Willow."

3. The story, a fantasy, was about tiny creatures from a hidden valley.

4. A visitor from the outside world, Milo, found the valley by accident.

5. The tiny Glen Willowans took him to Brustra IV, their queen.

6. The queen, a wise and kindly ruler, showed Milo the amazing kingdom.

B. Underline the appositive in each sentence. Then add commas where they are needed.

7. The lovely little valley was home to thousands of Glen Willowans all decendants of visitors from another planet.

8. The Glen Willowans peaceful and uninterested in the outside world lived happily in their little valley for thousands of years.

9. In fact, Milo a young boy from the city of Schenectady, New York, was the first human in the valley in all its history.

10. Milo loved the valley a place of peace, tranquility, and good fellowship among all creatures.

11. Glen Willowans, birds, animals, and even the plants all as tiny as the three-inch Glen Willowans themselves lived in perfect harmony.

12. Glen Willow a land without shouts or loud voices never had a war, a fight, or even an argument in all its history.

13. For several days, Milo toured the valley a land of great beauty.

14. On a nearby hill he saw Switherdon Falls a lovely waterfall and row after row of tiny pine trees.

15. At the end of the story, Milo sadly returned to the outside world his proper home.

Extension: Have students work in pairs to identify appositive words or phrases in sentences from their science or social studies books.

Name

Mechanics: Forming Possessive Nouns and Contractions

Use an apostrophe and *s* **('s)** to form the possessive of a singular noun and a plural noun that does not end in *s*.

the singer's poise   Gus's voice   the children's chorus

Use an apostrophe alone (') to form the possessive of a plural noun that ends in *s*.

the players' ability   the singers' mistakes

Use an apostrophe to replace one or more letters omitted in a contraction.

the orchestra is → the orchestra's

A. Write the possessive form of each noun below.

1. musician

2. Gracie

3. trumpets

4. glass

5. conductors

6. sonatas

7. audience

8. children

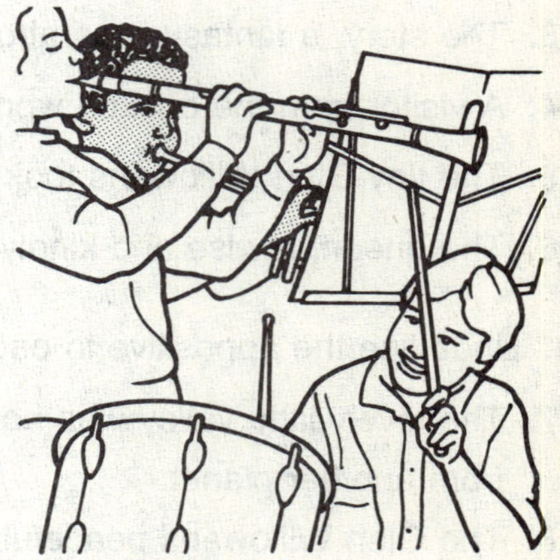

B. On the lines below, rewrite each incorrect sentence, changing apostrophes and/or adding the letter *s* as needed. Circle the numbers of any sentences that are correct.

9. Lane Schools known for its excellent music program.

10. The school's music department gives several concerts each year.

11. The orchestras fame has spread throughout the area.

12. The chorus' frequently is asked to perform in public.

13. This summer, the band's performing in Clayton Park every Wednesday evening.

Extension: Have students use the possessive nouns in Part A in sentences of their own.

Name ______________________________

Mechanics: Capitalizing Proper Nouns

A **proper noun** is a noun that names a particular person, place, thing, or idea. Capitalize all proper nouns.

Roberto Clemente	Madison Avenue
Town Hall	August

A. Write each proper noun using the correct capitalization.

1. jaimie ______________________
2. port washington ______________________
3. epcot center ______________________
4. mother's day ______________________
5. manhattan project ______________________
6. f.b.i. ______________________
7. statue of liberty ______________________
8. april ______________________

B. Capitalize each proper noun.

9. Herman melville, one of america's greatest writers, was born in new york city in 1819.
10. His family came from well-known colonial families originally from england and holland.
11. Melville's father, however, suffered financial misfortunes, and herman's family was left poor.
12. At the age of 20, young melville signed on as a seaman and sailed on a merchant ship to liverpool, england.
13. After teaching school for a while in upstate new york, melville set sail on the whaling ship *acushnet* in january 1841.
14. He hunted whales, worked on a merchant ship from australia, deserted the ship in tahiti and lived among natives of polynesia, and even served aboard the warship, *united states*.
15. On his return, melville wrote about his experiences in a book entitled *typee*.
16. The book was a success, and melville found himself one of america's most popular authors.
17. In later years, however, the writer fell from the favor of the reading public of both england and the united states.
18. His books, including the famous *moby dick,* a story about a giant white whale, were said to be too difficult and too philosophical.

Extension: Challenge students to write a paragraph using as many proper nouns as they can.

Name ____________________

Vocabulary Building: How Language Changes

Words come into the English language in many different ways.

A **clipped word** is a shortened form of a longer word.

necktie → tie   moving picture → movie

A **blend** is a word formed from the parts of other words.

smoke + fog → smog   parachute + sailing → parasailing

A **borrowed word** comes from a language other than English.

al-jebr (Arabic) → algebra   flamengo (Portuguese) → flamingo

Write whether each underlined word is a **clipped** word, a **blend**, or a **borrowed** word. Use a dictionary to help you.

1. ____________ The school carnival is this week.
2. ____________ The entire school is a flurry of activity.
3. ____________ In the auditorium, pop music will be performed.
4. ____________ Movies will be shown at various times.
5. ____________ Outside, a barbecue will be held.
6. ____________ Banjo music will accompany the food.
7. ____________ A stunt plane will perform many thrilling feats.
8. ____________ In one trick, it will twirl toward the ground.
9. ____________ A limo will bring special guests to the fair.
10. ____________ Celebrities will attend a lunch on Saturday.
11. ____________ Their fans will wait for them outside.
12. ____________ At night, flares will light up the area.
13. ____________ A local station will telecast parts of the fair.
14. ____________ Ponchos will be available in the event of rain.
15. ____________ Still, a visitor should bring along an umbrella.

Extension: Have students look in an unabridged dictionary to write the etymology of each of the underlined words on this page.

Name

Grammar and Writing Connection: Combining Sentences

You can use appositives to combine sentences. **Appositives**, or explanatory and identifying words and phrases, can be placed next to the words or names they tell about. If the appositive is not essential to explain the word clearly, it is set off by commas.

Rodrigo Diaz was Spain's greatest national hero. Diaz was called *El Cid*.
Rodrigo Diaz, *El Cid*, was Spain's greatest national hero.

When the appositive is essential to the meaning of the sentence, no comma is used.

The book *The Poem of the Cid* tells about this legendary Spanish hero.

Combine each pair of sentences by placing the identifying or explanatory words in the second sentence in the best place you can find in the first sentence. Use commas where they are needed.

1. El Cid fought against the enemies of Spain. These enemies were the Moors.

2. The Moors had invaded Spain many years before.
The Moors were Moslems from North Africa.

3. The name *El Cid* comes from the Arabic words *El Seid*.
The name *El Cid* means "the lord".

4. Rodrigo Diaz was El Cid. Rodrigo Diaz became famous in the eleventh century.

5. Diaz was a soldier of fortune.
Diaz fought for Arabian princes in northeastern Spain.

6. In the year 1094, he conquered the city of Valencia.
Valencia was a major fortress in the area.

7. Diaz and his armies attacked the Moors in nearby cities. Diaz was fierce.

Extension: Have students write two pairs of sentences. Then have students exchange papers and combine the sentences using appositives.

Name

Group Writing: A Short Story

A **short story** tells about people and events that have been created in the writer's imagination. It is written to entertain the people who read the story. Most short stories have three basic elements:

- **Plot:** The plot usually contains a conflict, or central problem, a high point, or climax, and a resolution, or solution, to the problem.
- **Characters:** These are the people who take part in the story's action.
- **Setting:** This is the time and place in which the story takes place.

A short story usually is divided into three parts: a **beginning**, which introduces the setting, characters, and conflict; a **middle**, which develops the plot; and an **ending**, which provides resolution to the conflict.

Dialogue, or conversation, helps to bring events and characters in the story to life.

Read this portion of a short story. Then answer the questions.

"I've just got to find it!" Joan called, pushing things this way and that in the top drawer of her dresser. "It's got to be here somewhere!"

Her friend Maria looked up. She was on her hands and knees, crawling out from under Joan's bed. "Well, it's not there," she said sadly. "Maybe it's not here at all."

"I know it is," Joan insisted. "Mom'll kill me if I don't find that car key. It's the only spare key we've got, and I put it in a special envelope so I wouldn't lose it. I always keep it right here in my room."

"Isn't there anything else we can do? I mean, your mother's stuck downtown, locked out of her car. Couldn't the police get into the car and bring her home?"

1. What is the setting of the story?

2. Who are the characters?

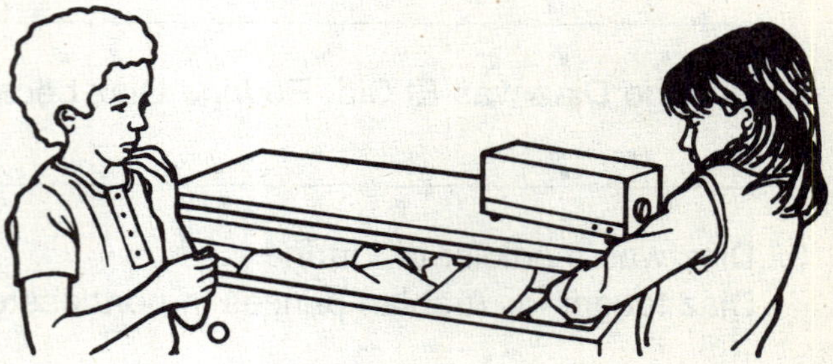

3. What is the problem or central conflict?

4. How do you think this story will end? What leads you to think this?

5. What is the term for conversation, when the characters speak in a story?

Extension: Have students analyze the elements of a favorite short story from their reader or other source.

Name ______________________

Thinking and Writing: Understanding Point of View

Every story is written from one of three **points of view**.

- **First Person:** The first person, "I," is the narrator. The narrator may be a person in the story or an outside observer and can tell only what he or she observes.
- **Third Person Limited:** The story is narrated from the point of view of a character in the story. The author reveals the thoughts and emotions of only this character, and understanding of other characters is limited to what this narrator sees, hears, and thinks to be true. The author uses the pronouns *he*, *she*, or *they*, or the characters' names.
- **Third Person Omniscient:** The narrator is all-knowing; the author can reveal the thoughts and motives of any character in the story.

Write **First Person**, **Third Person Limited**, or **Third Person Omniscient** to identify the point of view used in each story fragment.

1. We had been at sea for almost three days. During the whole time, our small boat had pitched and tossed on the ocean, making me feel terrible. My uncle, however, said that the bad weather would soon pass over. Then, he said, we would have clear sailing all the way to Hawaii. It was hard for me to believe, but I was glad to hope for something. The sailing trip from California to Hawaii was supposed to be fun!

   ____

2. Brad and Jason dug hastily, working as quickly as they could to dig a trench around their tent. Rain was pouring down heavily. They knew that their small tent soon would be completely flooded unless a trench could drain away the water. In minutes, the job was done, and they were back in the tent, drying themselves.

   ____

3. I stepped to the front of the stage. I had been practicing my solo for months, and I knew it perfectly. Still, I was nervous, and I hoped my nerves would settle down before I began. I looked up at the audience in the dark and smiled. Here goes, I thought.

   ____

4. Karen felt her blood pounding inside her as she moved along the track. The finish line was only a few yards away. Could she pass Brenda and win the race? Brenda felt her last strength failing. She didn't even see Karen drawing closer until she passed.

   ____

Extension: Have students rewrite one of the story fragments on this page from another point of view.

Name

Proofreading: Step 4

Indent ¶
Add ^
Add a comma ^,
Add quotation marks ^" ^"
Add a period ⊙
Take out
Capitalize ≡
Make a small letter /
Reverse the order

Read the following dialogue from a children's animal tale. See if the possessive forms of nouns are used correctly. Also, see if quotation marks are used correctly in the dialogue.

A. Mark changes and additions in the dialogue with proofreading marks from the box.

Look! hooted Alex Owl. Isn't that Felixs sister Felicia hopping down the trail?

I do believe those are Felicias ears, responded Olivia Owl.

Hopping closer, Felicia Rabbit said, Hello, Alex and Olivia. Do you know where my brothers den is located now?

It's over there, behind the childrens play area, answered Olivia. Do you need Alexs help with your bags?

No, thank you, folks, said Felicia. I'm just fine now that I'm within ten feet of my new home!

B. Use the changes and corrections you marked above to write the dialogue correctly on the lines below.

Name

Action Verbs

> An **action verb** is a word that expresses a physical or mental action.
> **Physical Action:** The pirates attacked the merchant ship at dawn.
> **Mental Action:** The ship expected the attack.

Underline the action verb in each sentence. Then circle the word that tells whether the verb describes **physical** or **mental** action.

1. Many infamous pirates terrorized the seas. physical mental
2. Notorious pirates in history included Edward Teach, or "Blackbeard." physical mental
3. His nickname came from his long black beard. physical mental
4. From 1716 to 1718, Blackbeard harassed the coasts of Virginia and North Carolina. physical mental
5. His ship, the *Queen Anne's Revenge*, assaulted any ship in its vicinity. physical mental
6. Teach's early life remains mysterious. physical mental
7. Blackbeard's appearance and actions added to his legend as a pirate. physical mental
8. He carried three braces, or pairs, of pistols. physical mental
9. He burned long matches under his hat during battles and attacks. physical mental
10. During peaceful times, he frightened his crew with pistol shots and fires. physical mental
11. Such antics made Blackbeard more terrifying than other pirates of the time. physical mental
12. According to legend, many planters from Virginia and North Carolina protected Blackbeard. physical mental
13. Finally, however, the planters turned on him. physical mental
14. In 1718, the governor of Virginia sent a British navy ship after the pirate. physical mental
15. Blackbeard finally died near Ocracoke Inlet, near Cape Hatteras, in North Carolina. physical mental

Extension: Challenge students to find out about another famous pirate and then write a short paragraph about him or her using action verbs in their sentences.

Name ______________________

Verbs with Direct Objects

The **direct object** is a noun or pronoun that receives the action of the verb. It can answer the question *whom?* or *what?* after an action verb.

Verb **Direct Object**

Divers explore the ocean floor.

A **transitive verb** is a verb that has a direct object.

The diver reached the shipwreck.

An **intransitive verb** is a verb that does not have a direct object.

The divers swam into the wreck.

Underline each action verb. Draw two lines under each direct object. Then write whether each verb is **transitive** or **intransitive.**

1. Jacques-Yves Cousteau explores the world of the sea. ______
2. His undersea adventures began in his youth. ______
3. In 1943, Cousteau helped with the design of the first aqualung. ______
4. This device freed divers of cumbersome diving suits. ______
5. Divers swam freely through the waters of the sea. ______
6. Cousteau's expeditions occur throughout the world. ______
7. He investigated ancient shipwrecks and sunken cities. ______
8. At other times, he looked at unusual creatures of the deep. ______
9. Today, Cousteau uses his ship *Calypso* for his explorations. ______
10. His activities include more than undersea expeditions. ______
11. He also creates books and movies about his discoveries. ______
12. His television series, *The Undersea World of Jacques Cousteau*, appeared for many years. ______
13. Cousteau used many techniques for underwater exploration. ______
14. He developed the aqualung, the first underwater diving station, and a diving saucer for undersea exploration. ______

Extension: Have students write four sentences that describe some of the actions performed by divers. Then have them underline the verb in each sentence, tell whether it is transitive or intransitive, and circle the direct object if there is one.

Name

Verbs with Indirect Objects

A **direct object** is a noun or pronoun that answers the question *whom?* or *what?* after an action verb. Sometimes an action verb is also followed by an indirect object. An **indirect object** answers the question *to whom? for whom? to what?* or *for what?* after an action verb.

Verb **Indirect Object** **Direct Object**

The guide gave my sister and me a tour.

Underline each action verb once, each direct object twice, and circle each indirect object.

1. Years ago, clipper ship designers gave the world a wonderful form of boat.
2. The graceful lines made these American ships fast.
3. Their speed brought merchants and customers goods more rapidly than ever before.
4. The "Baltimore Clippers" of Chesapeake Bay gave these ships their well-known name.
5. Enormous sails propelled the fast ships swiftly over the seas.
6. Their sleek lines helped the clippers in the water.
7. Clipper ships brought the American public goods from exotic places.
8. The clippers earned Americans many international sailing records.
9. The first clipper, the *Rainbow*, transformed John W. Griffiths into a noted ship designer.

10. *Flying Cloud*, perhaps the greatest clipper of all, made David McKay, its designer, famous.
11. Other clipper ships took captains and their crews to long-standing speed records.
12. Giant sails carried the *James Baines* from New York to England in just a little over twelve days.
13. A run of 465 miles in 24 hours gave the *Champion of the Seas* a record that lasted 25 years.
14. Square-rigged ships gradually replaced the graceful clipper ships.
15. Greater cargo space in the slower square-riggers offered their owners more profit.

Extension: Have students work in pairs to identify the indirect objects in sentences from newspapers or magazines.

Name

Linking Verbs

A **linking verb** tells what the subject of a sentence is or is like. A linking verb connects the subject of a sentence with a noun or an adjective in the predicate. The most common linking verbs are forms of the verb *be*.

A **predicate noun** follows a linking verb. It renames the subject, telling what the subject is.

Linking Verb ↓ (is) **Predicate Noun** ↓ (spot)

The seashore is my favorite vacation spot.

A **predicate adjective** follows a linking verb. It describes the subject, telling what the subject is like.

Linking Verb ↓ (feels) **Predicate Adjective** ↓ (wonderful)

The warm summer sun feels especially wonderful today.

Underline the linking verb in each sentence. Write and label each **predicate noun** and **predicate adjective** on the blank.

1. Cape Cod seems a wonderful place. ______________________
2. It is a sandy spit of land. ______________________
3. The surf sounds strong. ______________________
4. The fine white sand feels powdery. ______________________
5. People become tan in the sun. ______________________
6. The birds overhead are gulls. ______________________
7. The fresh seafood tastes delicious. ______________________
8. Those visitors appear happy. ______________________
9. The early settlers were whalers. ______________________
10. The sky looks dark now. ______________________
11. Cape Hatteras is another famous vacation spot. ______________________
12. In hurricane season, the seas become stormy. ______________________
13. Today, the area seems peaceful most of the time. ______________________
14. Tourists feel relaxed in the sun and surf of the Cape. ______________________
15. Visitors often become explorers of the place. ______________________

Extension: Have students write five sentences describing what they might see during a walk by the seashore. Have them use a different linking verb in each sentence.

Name

Present, Past, and Future Tenses

The **present tense** of a verb shows an action that happens at this moment or repeatedly.

Underwater archaeologists explore many places and things.

The **past tense** shows an action that already happened.

The ship submerged almost two thousand years ago.

The **future tense** shows an action that will take place in the future.

The divers will investigate the wreck for several weeks.

Underline each verb. Then, write whether it is in the **present, past,** or **future** tense.

1. Archaeologists often explore underwater sites. ____________
2. A few years ago, archaeologists discovered an ancient Greek ship under the sea. ____________
3. The ship rested in several hundred feet of water. ____________
4. Divers carried valuable artifacts back up to the surface. ____________
5. Afterwards, archaeologists on land will study the discoveries thoroughly. ____________
6. Divers used other methods in different locations. ____________
7. At some sites, giant vacuums scooped old coins and other artifacts up to the surface. ____________
8. Elsewhere, underwater archaeologists investigate ancient cities now under the sea. ____________
9. With the aid of aerial photography and sonar scanners they reveal sunken harbors and towns. ____________
10. Other electronic devices soon will assist archaeologists in their efforts. ____________

Extension: Have students write six sentences about a favorite music or television performer. Have them write two of the sentences in the present tense, two in the past tense, and two in the future tense.

Name ______________________________

Verb Phrases

Every verb has four principal parts: the **present**, the **present participle**, the **past**, and the **past participle**.

Present	**Present Participle**	**Past**	**Past Participle**
work	(is) working	worked	(has) worked

A **verb phrase** is formed by combining a principal part of a verb with a **helping verb**. In a verb phrase, the word that expresses the main action is called the **main verb**.

Verb Phrase

Present Participle: The boat is already pulling away from the dock.

Helping Verb **Main Verb**

Verb Phrase

Past Participle: Passengers have moved into their cabins.

Helping Verb **Main Verb**

A. Circle the correct helping verb in the parentheses. Then underline each verb phrase.

1. Jamie's parents (are, have) taking an ocean cruise this week.
2. They (are, have) traveled on ships several times before.
3. On those trips they (are, have) journeyed to Florida to meet their ship.
4. For this trip, they (are, have) boarding in New York City.
5. Their new plans (are, have) making this trip much easier.

B. Underline the correct helping verb in parentheses. Then circle each main verb.

6. The ship (is, has) leaving just after noon, today.
7. The passengers (are, have) already standing on the dock.
8. The passengers (are, have) waited patiently to go on board.
9. The crew (is, has) helping with the arrangements.
10. The ship's staff (is has) welcomed them to the ship.
11. The crew (is, has) loaded passengers' luggage and ship's supplies.
12. The ship's giant propellers (are, have) already turning.
13. With a shout, the crew (is, has) tossed free the ship's lines.

Extension: Have students tell whether the main verb in each of the sentences in Part B is the present or past participle.

Name ______________________________

Present and Past Progressive Forms

The **present progressive** form of a verb expresses an action that is continuing in the present. It consists of the present participle of the main verb and the helping verb *am, is,* or *are.*

The boat is racing across the lake right now.

The **past progressive** form expresses an action that continued for some time in the past. It consists of the present participle of the main verb and the helping verb *was* or *were.*

Our friends were waterskiing for three hours yesterday.

A. Underline the verb phrases. Then write whether each verb phrase is in the **present progressive** or the **past progressive.**

1. Boating is becoming more popular than ever. ____________
2. Many people are enjoying the fun and excitement of boats. ____________
3. Others are trying such challenging sports as waterskiing. ____________
4. In days gone by, many people were using their boats just for fishing. ____________
5. Sailboat owners often were sailing their boats from place to place for an entire weekend. ____________

B. Complete each sentence. Write the verb in parentheses in the form that is shown.

6. Many powerboat owners ____________ up and down America's long rivers. (travel; present progressive)
7. Regardless of their activities, boat owners ____________ a wonderful time with their boats. (have; present progressive)
8. Paula and Vera ____________ the gasoline, the life preservers, and the other gear carefully. (check; past progressive)
9. In minutes, they ____________ their way from the dock. (ease; past progressive)
10. Soon they ____________ back and forth across the lake. (dash; past progressive)
11. For some time, Paula ____________ tricks on waterskis. (perform; past progressive)

Extension: Have students work in pairs to identify the present progressive and past progressive forms of verbs in sentences in their reader or social studies text.

Name

Perfect Tenses

The **present perfect tense** of a verb expresses an action that began at some indefinite time in the past and may continue into the present. It uses the helping verb *has* or *have.*

The class has studied the history of steamships.
I have studied the history of steamships for at least a year.

The **past perfect tense** expresses an action that began and ended before another past action began. It uses the helping verb *had.*

Before now, the class had studied other great inventions.

The **future perfect tense** expresses an action that will have begun and ended by the time that another future action begins. It uses the helping verbs *will* or *shall* and *have.*

By Friday, the class will have finished the work on steamships.

A. Underline each verb phrase. Then write whether each verb is in the **present perfect, past perfect,** or **future perfect** tense.

1. By next week, our class will have learned a great deal about steamboats. ______
2. Gina has researched John Fitch, the inventor of the first steamboat. ______
3. Her report has revealed interesting facts about Fitch. ______
4. The teacher had prepared pictures of Fitch's early steamboat for us to see. ______
5. By 1790, Fitch had established regular steamboat service between Philadelphia, Pennsylvania, and Burlington, New Jersey. ______

B. Write the tense of the verb indicated in parentheses.

6. He ______ steamboats before then, however. (construct; past perfect)
7. We also ______ the work of Robert Fulton, a more famous inventor. (study; present perfect)
8. Fulton ______ his adult life as a painter. (start; past perfect)
9. He always ______ new and unusual inventions, however. (create; past perfect)

Extension: Have students write six sentences about something they did on a class outing. Have them use a verb in the present perfect, past perfect, or future perfect tense in each sentence.

Name ______________________________

Irregular Verbs I

To form the past tense and the past participle of most verbs, you just add *ed* or *d*. **Irregular verbs** are different. To form the past tense of an irregular verb, you have to change the spelling of the word. Sometimes there is a spelling change when an irregular verb is changed from the past to the past participle form.

Verb	Past	Past Participle
do	did	(have, has, had) done
run	ran	(have, has, had) run
sing	sang	(have, has, had) sung
buy	bought	(have, has, had) bought

Read each sentence. Then write the correct form of the verb in parentheses to complete the sentence.

1. Mr. Edmonds has ______________ us many things about the pond behind our house. (teach)
2. Some of us have ______________ by the water's edge for hours at a time. (sit)
3. Last week, several deer ______________ from the cool waters of the pond. (drink)
4. They ______________ quickly away at the sound of our approach. (run)
5. We have ______________ several unusual kinds of fish there, too. (catch)
6. Some ______________ from the water in wonderful leaps and jumps. (spring)
7. Birds have ______________ their lovely songs there for many years. (sing)
8. Mr. Edmonds ______________ us some jars to hold water samples from the pond. (lend)
9. We ______________ the clear jars up to the light in the kitchen. (hold)
10. Hundreds of tiny organisms ______________ in the water from the pond. (swim)
11. Mr. Edmonds has ______________ many interesting specimens up from the pond. (bring)
12. We ______________ a microscope for the water samples from the pond. (buy)
13. We have ______________ of several science projects about the pond. (think)
14. Brian has ______________ a scale model of the pond. (make)
15. We have ______________ many good projects for this coming summer. (leave)

Extension: Have students write the correct past tense of the verbs *bring, buy, lose, pay,* and *seek* to write five sentences about a trip to a shopping mall.

Name

Irregular Verbs II

Remember these rules when you want to change an **irregular verb** from its past to its **past participle** form.

To form the past participle of some irregular verbs, add an *n* to the verb itself.

grow → (have, has, had) grown **drive → (have, has, had) driven**

Some past participles are formed by adding an *n* to the past form of the verb.

broke → (have, has, had) broken **woke → (have, has, had) woken**

Some irregular verbs do not follow any rules.

go → went → (have, has, had) gone **ride → rode → (have, has, had) ridden**

A. Write the past tense and past participle of each verb.

Verb	Past Tense	Past Participle
1. speak		
2. drive		
3. know		
4. write		
5. throw		
6. freeze		
7. fly		

B. Write each sentence, using the tense of the verb indicated in parentheses.

8. We _____ wonderful plays at the Playhouse. (see; past participle)

9. The actors _____ lovely costumes. (wear; past)

10. The shows _____ enthusiastic audiences. (draw; past participle)

11. The audience _____ the performers standing ovations. (give; past)

Extension: Have students write five sentences, leaving blanks where the verbs should be. Then have students exchange papers, and fill in the correct past or past participle form of the missing verb.

Name ______________________________

Subject-Verb Agreement

A verb must agree in number with its subject.
Use a singular verb with a singular subject and a plural verb with a plural subject.

Singular: The island of Tahiti lies in the South Seas. It has attracted many visitors over the years.

Plural: Visitors enjoy its beauty and climate. They call it the "Paradise of the Pacific."

A verb must agree with the subject even if the verb comes before the subject or the verb is separated from the subject by other words.

Singular	**Plural**
Has he seen the pictures?	Have they seen the pictures?
There is a coral reef.	There are rugged mountains.
The coral reef around the island is spectacular.	The waterfalls in the mountain areas are spectacular, too.

A. Underline the correct form of the verb for each sentence.

1. People in Tahiti (comes, come) from many places.
2. The island (has, have) many Polynesians.
3. There (is, are) also many French and Chinese Tahitians.
4. Many people (lives, live) between the mountains and shore.
5. (Has, Have) he read anything about the island's history?
6. The people of the island (grow, grows) many products.
7. There (is, are) many acres of coconuts and sugar cane.
8. Other products (includes, include) vanilla and pearls.
9. Tahiti's beauty (has, have), over the years, inspired many artists.
10. The island, with its beauty, (is, are) known from paintings.

B. Complete each sentence with the correct form of the verb.

11. Vinnie, one of my classmates, ____________ the author of a report on Tahiti. (is, are)
12. People in the class ____________ his report. (enjoys, enjoy)
13. ____________ students like such reports? (Does, Do)
14. Mrs. Richards, one of our favorite teachers, ____________ to Tahiti on a map. (points, point)
15. Students ____________ attention to her. (pays, pay)

Extension: Have students underline the subject in each of the sentences on this page. Then have students tell whether the subjects and verbs are plural or singular.

Name ______________________

Mechanics: Using Commas to Separate Parts of a Sentence

Use **commas** to separate three or more **items in a series.**

Ketches, catamarans, and sunfish are popular sailboats today.

Use **commas** to show a pause after an **introductory word.**

Yes, I enjoy sailing.

Use **commas** to set off a group of **words that interrupt the flow of thought.**

Karen Olsen, I think, is the owner of a boat.

Use **commas** to set off nouns of **direct address.**

Please, Nora, will you take us sailing?

A. Read each sentence. If its use of commas is correct, write **correct**. If a comma or commas are missing, add commas where needed.

__________ **1.** For thousands of years, boats have traveled by sail.

__________ **2.** Today's sailboats are I think some of the most exciting in history.

__________ **3.** Boston, Cleveland, San Diego, and Miami are on the water.

__________ **4.** Jorge didn't you take sailing lessons last summer?

__________ **5.** People often feel excited and refreshed after a day on a sailboat.

__________ **6.** A person first starting to sail I remember feels awkward and ill-at-ease.

__________ **7.** Yes Joe the novice sailor soon begins to feel at home with the boat.

__________ **8.** There are many different types of boats available for today's part-time or amateur sailor.

B. Add commas where needed.

9. Many people including me prefer small open sailboats.

10. My best friends and I rode our bikes parked and locked them and rode the subway to get to our sailing lessons.

11. Doris you became our most fearless sailor.

12. Luckily you were there to help me right the boat when I capsized.

13. Today's fiberglass boats are easier to turn upright and unfortunately to tip over.

14. Boating is hard work exciting and fun.

15. Many cities I bet have sailing lessons available to the public.

Extension: Have students explain why commas were needed in the sentences in Part B.

Name ______________________________

Vocabulary Building: Word Choice

The **denotation** of a word is its exact, literal meaning. The **connotation** of a word is the positive or negative impression, or mental picture, that it conveys. Words can have similar meanings but different connotations.

Positive Connotation: Mark decided to fix the boat.
Negative Connotation: Mark decided to overhaul the boat.

A. Write the word in each group that has a positive connotation.

1. shout	call	yell	______________
2. gaze	spy	stare	______________
3. stun	surprise	flabbergast	______________
4. work	toil	labor	______________
5. chilly	refreshing	frigid	______________
6. devour	consume	dine	______________
7. curious	nosy	prying	______________
8. glaring	gleaming	blinding	______________

B. Underline the word in parentheses that gives each sentence a negative connotation.

9. Last summer, Mark discovered a (shabby, weathered) boat near the lake.
10. He planned to (renovate, renew) it in time for summer.
11. The job took hours of (painstaking, hard) work.
12. Mark was (choosy, fussy) about the new parts for the boat.
13. Finally, the (task, chore) was completed.
14. Mark and his friends took the boat to the (busy, crowded) dock.
15. They (launched, shoved) it into the (calm, motionless) water.

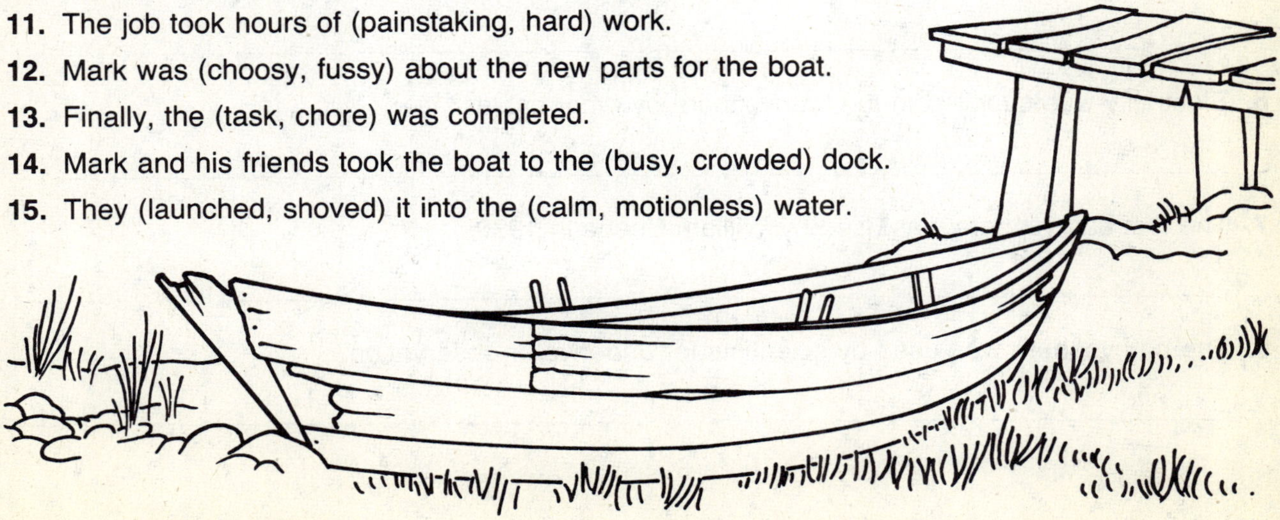

Extension: Have students work in pairs to develop a list of five words whose connotation is positive. Then have students exchange papers with another student pair and list similar words that have a negative connotation.

Name

Grammar and Writing Connection: Using Active and Passive Voices

When the verb is in the **active voice**, the subject of the sentence performs the action.

The sea has fascinated people.

Scientists use many devices in the study of the sea.

When the verb is in the **passive voice**, the subject receives the action of the verb.

People have been fascinated by the sea.

Many devices are used by scientists in the study of the sea.

Use verbs in the active voice to make your writing strong and direct. Avoid overusing the passive voice.

Rewrite these sentences by changing each passive verb to the active voice.

1. An important device was invented by scientists in the 1930s.

2. The device was called the *bathysphere* by its inventors.

3. The bathysphere was given a round shape by its designers.

4. Large windows for good visibility were added by the builders.

5. The bathysphere was lowered from a ship by heavy steel cables.

6. Electricity was supplied to the bathysphere by other cables.

7. The first bathysphere was used by William Beebe in 1930.

8. The bathysphere was used by scientists for underwater observation.

Extension: Have students write five sentences using verbs in the passive voice. Then have students exchange papers and rewrite the sentences by changing the verb to the active voice.

PRACTICE-39

Name

Group Writing: An Explanatory Paragraph

An **explanation** informs your readers or listeners. When you write an **explanatory paragraph**, you tell someone how something works or how to do something. A good explanation begins with a **topic sentence** that tells what the paragraph will be about. It also uses **details** to develop or support the topic sentence. These details can be **organized** in **chronological order, order of importance,** or even by **comparison and contrast.** An explanation uses **transition words** to link the details together, and it contains a **concluding sentence** that often summarizes the information you have presented.

Read the paragraph below. Then answer the questions that follow.

(1) Dogs make wonderful pets, and, when owners follow a few simple guidelines, dogs can be easy to care for. (2) Food, for example, is not difficult to provide for most dogs. (3) Adult dogs need only a single meal each day, although a light meal might be given in the morning in addition. (4) Meat generally is recommended for the larger meal, with milk and vegetables for lighter meals. (5) While dogs do not need to eat constantly, they should have as much drinking water as possible. (6) Also, they should be provided with shelter from cold weather, drafts, and dampness. (7) Finally, dogs need basic grooming. (8) Dogs do not need to be bathed often, but they do need to be brushed and combed frequently. (9) In the same way, they need regular professional care of their teeth, nails, and gums. (10) None of this is very complicated—or very time-consuming. (11) In fact, a few moments a day are all that may be needed to care for our "best friend."

1. What is the topic of this paragraph? ______

2. What is the number of the topic sentence? ______

3. What transition words are used in the paragraph? ______

______

4. What supporting details are given? ______

______

5. Which sentence presents the conclusion? ______

Extension: Have students find an example of an explanatory paragraph in their science textbooks and then identify its topic sentence, supporting details, transition words, and concluding sentence.

Name

Thinking and Writing: Comparing and Contrasting

Explanations can show the similarities and differences between two things. A **comparison** shows the similarities between things. A **contrast** shows the differences between them. When you compare and contrast things, there are different ways you can arrange your information.

- You can present all the details about one subject first, and then give details about the other subject.
- You can present the similarities or differences point by point, alternating between the two subjects.

Read the paragraph, and then answer the questions that follow.

Classical ballet and modern dance are the two most popular forms of dancing in performance. Ballet began as far back as the Middle Ages, and in the 1500s the King of France, Louis XIV, founded the Royal Academy of Dance and Music to train professional dancers in technical skills. Since then, ballet became more and more formal and added dancing "on point." This difficult toe dancing has become ballet's current trademark. Modern dance, in contrast, is less formal. Founded at the beginning of the twentieth century, modern dance encourages the dancer to create his or her own patterns and style. Unlike the ballet dancer, the modern dancer uses his or her entire body, often in large or unusual movements. The founder of modern dance, Isadora Duncan, was inspired by the art and thought of ancient Greece. Other founders of modern dance, such as Ruth St. Denis, turned to the Far East for inspiration. Since their time, the modern dance movement has grown stronger and stronger, and now occupies as central a place in audiences' hearts as does classical ballet.

1. Is this a paragraph of comparison or contrast? ____________________

2. What similarities are described? ____________________

3. What differences are described? ____________________

____

____

____

4. What transition words are used in the paragraph? ____________________

5. What does the concluding sentence tell you? ____________________

____

Extension: Have students choose items to contrast and compare and then make notes on how their subjects are similar or different.

Name

Proofreading: Step 4

Indent ¶
Add ^
Add a comma ^,
Add quotation marks ‟ ”
Add a period ⊙
Take out
Capitalize ≡
Make a small letter /
Reverse the order

Read this section of a script for an action-adventure movie. Check to see whether the verb tenses are used correctly. Also, check to see whether commas are used wherever they are needed.

A. Use the proofreading marks from the box to mark corrections or additions to the script.

Brett: Well I'm hoped we're the only ones in this old crypt, Kana.

Kana: Yes Brett. We are I believe the only ones here. I have hoped however to find more than just stone walls today.

Brett: We had been here for an hour soon I think Kana. We had bumped crawled and scraped enough for one day.

Kana: Brett look! A strange blue-green light is shined through a crack in that far wall. We has passed it before, but we must have miss it.

Brett: Oh no! I had seen that look on your face before partner. I am feel sorry already!

B. Use the corrections and additions you marked above to write the script correctly.

PRACTICE-42

Name

Personal Pronouns

A **pronoun** is a word that takes the place of a noun or nouns.

John practices hard. He is a great athlete.

Personal pronouns are pronouns that refer primarily to persons.
Use a **subject pronoun** when the pronoun is the subject of the sentence. *I*, *you*, *he*, *she*, *it*, *we*, and *they* are subject pronouns.

They are members of my team.

Use an **object pronoun** when it is the object of a verb or the object of a preposition. *We, you, him, her, it, us*, and *them* are object pronouns.

We gave them uniforms for him.

Write the pronoun you would use in place of the underlined word or words in each sentence.

1. ______________ Jim Thorpe was one of history's great athletes.
2. ______________ This athlete was born in Oklahoma in 1888.
3. ______________ Thorpe was a descendant of Black Hawk, a warrior and chief of the Sauk tribe.
4. ______________ Thorpe's football performances put the Carlisle Indian Industrial School on the athletic map.
5. ______________ These performances won him all-American honors in 1911 and 1912.
6. ______________ In 1912, the young man competed in several events in the Olympic Games.
7. ______________ He won the decathlon and pentathlon.
8. ______________ Later, officials stripped Thorpe of the awards.
9. ______________ In 1913, Thorpe played baseball professionally.
10. ______________ His abilities thrilled fans at every ballpark.
11. ______________ After this, Thorpe turned to a career in professional football.
12. ______________ This career made Thorpe a legendary athlete.

Extension: Have students write **S** above each subject pronoun on this page and **O** above each object pronoun.

Name

Pronouns and Antecedents

The nouns or noun that a pronoun replaces is called the pronoun's **antecedent**. A pronoun must always **agree** with its antecedent in **number** (singular or plural) and **gender** (masculine, feminine, or neuter).

Masculine Singular Antecedent — **Masculine Singular Pronoun**

Henry David Thoreau was a writer and thinker. He was born in 1817.

Complete each sentence by writing the correct pronoun. Then circle its antecedent.

1. Thoreau graduated from Harvard College in 1837. ________________ was twenty years old.
2. After graduating from Harvard, Thoreau was a schoolteacher, but then ________________ turned to performing odd jobs to support himself.
3. At that time, Thoreau met the writer Ralph Waldo Emerson and his wife. ________________ befriended and helped the young man.
4. The Emersons encouraged Thoreau to write. They even employed ________________ as a gardener for a short time.
5. In 1845, Thoreau built a small hut on Walden Pond. ________________ lived there from July 4, 1845, to September 6, 1847.
6. Thoreau's book *Walden* describes many experiences and thoughts. ________________ occurred at Walden Pond.
7. A simple, natural life is praised in the book. Over the years, ________________ has inspired thousands of people.
8. *Walden* is considered to be an American classic, but translations of ________________ appear in countries all over the world.
9. Thoreau wrote "Civil Disobedience" in 1849. In this work, ________________ argued that people should not support laws they do not believe in.
10. This work was thought to be Thoreau's most important essay. ________________ influenced Gandhi in his campaign against British rule in India.

Extension: Have students write three pairs of sentences about the main character in a book they have read. The second sentence in each pair should have a pronoun that refers to its antecedent.

Name

Using Pronouns Correctly

If a pronoun is part of a **compound subject,** use a subject pronoun. If a pronoun is part of a **compound object,** use an object pronoun. Use the pronoun *I* or *me* last in a compound subject or object.

Subject Pronoun ↓ Thomas and she fixed the tennis net.

Object Pronoun ↓ Mrs. Lu thanked Thomas and her.

Use the subject pronoun after a linking verb in formal writing.

Subject Pronoun ↓ Alicia's first opponent was she.

Write the correct pronoun or pronouns from the choices in parentheses.

1. Vera and (I, me) love tennis more than anything else. ____
2. (I and Vera, Vera and I) have been taking tennis lessons for several years. ____
3. This year, Coach Leonard has been giving (we, us) special lessons. ____
4. That is (he, him) over there, the man in the blue warm-up suit. ____
5. (He, Him) and Mr. Waters play doubles with us every Thursday. ____
6. Coach Leonard has entered Vera and (I, me) in several matches. ____
7. (We, Us) will play other teams from all over this area. ____
8. The best doubles team, though, is (we, us). ____
9. Coach Leonard expects (we, us) to win the division championship this year. ____
10. (I and Vera, Vera and I) will work especially hard this year. ____
11. Our friends told Vera and (I, me) they would cheer us on. ____
12. I told (them, they) we would appreciate that. ____
13. (Them, They) and our other classmates will come. ____
14. The other team is probably just like (we, us), though. ____
15. (They and we, Them and us) both want to win. ____

Extension: Have students circle all subject pronouns on this page and underline each object pronoun.

Name ______________________________

Possessive Pronouns

A **possessive noun** is a word that names who or what has something. A **possessive pronoun** can take the place of a possessive noun. Possessive pronouns can come before a noun or stand alone.

Yuriko's experiment was exciting. **(Possessive Noun)**

Her science project was the best. **(Possessive Pronoun)**

Mine earned the second prize. **(Possessive Pronoun)**

Possessive pronouns do not use apostrophes. Do not confuse contractions, such as *you're, it's, they're,* and *there's* with possessive pronouns.

You're going to have fun when you do your own science project.

Underline the possessive noun in each sentence. Then write the possessive pronoun you should use to replace that noun.

______________ **1.** Ryan's class is having a science fair this week.

______________ **2.** The students' projects will be displayed in the gym.

______________ **3.** Mark and Gina's project is about electricity.

______________ **4.** Mrs. Smith's committee will judge the projects.

______________ **5.** Doreen pointed to the atomic energy display and said, "That is Doreen's."

______________ **6.** Nora told Betty, "Betty's project will surely win."

______________ **7.** The teachers asked Josh about Josh's project.

______________ **8.** People's projects were set up the day before.

______________ **9.** Everyone crowded into the gym on the science fair's opening day.

______________ **10.** That project about animal habitats is Martha and Cara's.

______________ **11.** "Mona," Dr. Smithson said to me, "the best exhibit is Mona's."

______________ **12.** Philip's display showed the inner workings of ears.

______________ **13.** The idea for the project was completely Philip's.

______________ **14.** Vicki conducted tests about human taste buds for Vicki's project.

______________ **15.** Sara and Calla put Sara and Calla's project under the window.

Extension: Have students write six sentences containing possessive nouns. Then have students exchange papers and substitute possessive pronouns for the possessive nouns.

Name ______________________________

Indefinite Pronouns

An **indefinite pronoun** is a pronoun that does not refer to a specific person, place, or thing. The following indefinite pronouns are always singular: *each, either, neither, anyone, anybody, someone, somebody, something, one, everything, everyone, everybody, everything, nobody, nothing, no one.*

These indefinite pronouns are always plural: *few, many, several, both, others.*

These indefinite pronouns can be either singular or plural: *all, any, most, none, some.*

Possessive pronouns must agree with their antecedents in gender and number. When the antecedent is a singular indefinite pronoun whose gender is not specified, use the masculine and feminine singular possessive pronoun.

Singular (Everyone) **Singular** (his, her) **Plural** (Many) **Plural** (their)

Everyone has his or her favorite team. Many cheered their team on.

Write the pronoun or pronouns that are needed to complete each sentence.

1. Nobody wanted to miss _____ chance to go to the game. ____________
2. Everybody was looking forward to _____ favorite event. ____________
3. To our surprise, someone gave us _____ tickets. ____________
4. Karen and I said, "These tickets are _____ now." ____________
5. When Janet and Sue won tickets, neither could believe _____ good fortune. ____________
6. Several asked us to buy _____ tickets for them. ____________
7. However, no one could have purchased _____ tickets so late. ____________
8. Some came early, hoping to improve _____ luck. ____________
9. Something exciting was having _____ effect that day. ____________
10. All of the spectators were hurrying to _____ seats. ____________
11. Many made _____ entrance just at the sound of the buzzer. ____________
12. When the players came on, I held _____ breath. ____________
13. Everyone had soon taken _____ place on the field. ____________
14. Others who were late had missed _____ chance. ____________
15. Everybody jumped to _____ feet and cheered. ____________

Extension: Have students underline the indefinite pronouns on this page.

Name ______________________

Subject-Verb Agreement with Indefinite Pronouns

Singular indefinite pronoun subjects take singular verbs. Plural indefinite pronoun subjects take plural verbs.

Singular → Everyone; **Singular** → has

Everyone in my class has heard of Mount Everest.

Plural → Most; **Plural** → dream

Most (people) dream of climbing to its peak.

With indefinite pronouns that can be singular or plural, look at the phrase that follows the pronoun to decide whether to use a singular or plural verb.

Some of the attempts have been successful.

Each of the attempts has been heroic.

Write the verb in parentheses that agrees with the subject.

1. Many ______________ dreamed of climbing Mount Everest, the tallest mountain in the world. (has, have)
2. Few ______________ ever actually accomplished this difficult feat. (has, have)
3. It was not until 1953 that anyone ______________ able to reach the top of this mountain. (was, were)
4. No one ______________ expecting Edmund Hillary and his Sherpa guide, Tenzing Norgay, to reach the top. (was, were)
5. Everyone ______________ overjoyed at their amazing accomplishment. (was, were)
6. Even today, some ______________ to climb this amazing peak. (fails, fail)
7. Others, however, ______________ fame with their efforts. (achieves, achieve)
8. In 1956, for example, someone from a Swiss expedition ______________ able to climb Mount Everest twice. (was, were)
9. In 1963, others, part of an American expedition, ______________ successful. (was, were)
10. None, however, ______________ achieved the fame of Hillary and Norgay, the first conquerors of the world's highest mountain. (has, have)

Extension: Have students write five sentences containing indefinite pronouns, leaving blanks where the verbs should be. Then have students exchange papers and fill in the correct verbs.

Name

Reflexive and Intensive Pronouns

A **reflexive pronoun** directs the action of the verb back to the subject.

Years ago, many people found themselves suffering from yellow fever.

An **intensive pronoun** adds emphasis to a noun or pronoun already named.

Many American doctors themselves had suffered from the disease.

Do not use a reflexive or an intensive pronoun where a subject or an object pronoun belongs.

Larry and ~~myself~~ I will study it. He asked ~~myself~~ me to help him.

Hisself, theirselves, and *ourself* should be avoided; they are never correct.

Write the correct pronoun from the parentheses.

1. In the early 1900s, a young American army doctor made ________________ famous for his work with yellow fever. (him, himself)
2. Walter Reed and his research team acquainted ________________ firsthand with this dangerous disease. (theirselves, themselves)
3. In 1898, Reed ________________ conducted experiments on the causes of yellow fever. (hisself, himself)
4. Healthy volunteers were needed to submit ________________ to the bite of a mosquito infected with yellow fever. (them, themselves)
5. In 1900, part of Reed's team allowed ________________ to be infected with the disease. (it, itself)
6. The experiments cost ________________ dearly. (them, themselves)
7. One doctor allowed ________________ to be infected, and he nearly died of the disease. (him, himself)
8. These experiments convinced ________________ that mosquitoes carried the disease from person to person. (him, himself)
9. The experiments with yellow fever, however, taught doctors how to control ________________. (it, itself)
10. Because of the work of the doctors and volunteers ________________, future epidemics of yellow fever were prevented. (them, themselves)
11. Walter Reed ________________ died in 1902 from chronic appendicitis. (him, himself)

Extension: Have students write five sentences about a sport or game they played. Have students use one of these pronouns in each sentence: *myself, herself, himself, itself,* or *ourselves.*

Name ______________________________

Interrogative and Demonstrative Pronouns

An **interrogative pronoun** is a pronoun that introduces an interrogative sentence. *Who, whom, whose, which,* and *what* can be used as interrogative pronouns.

What did he read? Who was that? Whose are those? Which do you like?

A **demonstrative pronoun** is a pronoun that points out something and stands alone in a sentence. *This, that, these,* and *those* are demonstrative pronouns.

This is the one I like. Those are interesting books.

Do not confuse the interrogative pronoun *whose* with *who's,* which is the contraction of *who is.*

Who's Louis Braille? He was a student whose invention allowed the blind to read.

A. Write the word from the parentheses that correctly completes the sentence.

1. (What, That) is the Braille system? ____________
2. For (who, whom) was it developed? ____________
3. (These, What) are books written in Braille. ____________
4. (Whose, Who's) are they? ____________
5. How do you think blind people read (whose, these)? ____________
6. (Those, Which) are raised dots that make up an alphabet. ____________
7. (Who's, Whose) fingers can feel the patterns of the dots? ____________

B. Underline the interrogative pronouns once and the demonstrative pronouns twice.

8. Who developed this for blind people?
9. Did you know Louis Braille invented this?
10. That was an amazing discovery for a fifteen-year-old boy.
11. What caused Louis Braille's own blindness?
12. Who inspired Braille's system?
13. That was not Braille's first attempt at a reading system.
14. Do you know whom I should ask about this?
15. What led a French schoolboy to this discovery?
16. These were the other inventions that helped Louis Braille with his idea.

Extension: Have students write *interrogative* or *demonstrative* above or beside each pronoun they wrote in Part A.

Name

Mechanics: Using Abbreviations

An **abbreviation** is the shortened form of a word.

Some abbreviations begin with a capital letter and end with a period.

Mon. (Monday), Jan. (January), Ave. (Avenue)

Abbreviations for titles and times place periods after each capital letter.

M.D. (Medical Doctor), A.M. (ante-meridian)

Other abbreviations use capital letters and no periods.

NBC (National Broadcasting Company), MN (Minnesota)

Units of measure do not use capital letters but do use periods.

ft. (foot), lb. (pound), pt. (pint)

A. Find the word or words that can be abbreviated in each item. Write the abbreviation.

1. six inches

2. Buffalo, New York

3. 9:00 at night

4. Sam Wilson, Registered Nurse

5. Tuesday bus schedule

6. Hilton Washington, Junior

7. Crane Media, Incorporated

8. Los Alamos Boulevard

B. Find the word or words in each sentence that can be abbreviated. Then rewrite the sentence using the correct abbreviation.

9. Doctor Gina Riccardi announced a new hospital program this week.

10. A film of the program will be shown on the local Columbia Broadcasting Company station tomorrow night.

Extension: Have students look through magazine and newspaper articles, cookbooks, and instruction books to list abbreviations that they find.

PRACTICE-51

Name ______________________________

Vocabulary Building: Homophones and Homographs

Homophones are words that sound alike but have different spellings and different meanings.

ate (did eat)	buy (purchase)	board (lumber)
eight (number)	by (near)	bored (uninterested)

Homographs are words that are spelled the same but have different meanings and sometimes different pronunciations.

hide (conceal)	fast (quick)	close (near)
hide (animal skin)	fast (stop eating)	close (shut)

A. Choose the correct homophone from the parentheses.

1. The team will do ____________ best in the championship game. (it's, its)

2. Do you know ____________ the best player on the entire team? (who's, whose)

3. Please bring ____________ ticket with you. (your, you're)

4. The Hornets ____________ the last game between the two teams. (one, won)

5. ____________ were the first goals scored? (Who's, Whose)

6. The players played ____________ best game of the season. (their, they're, there)

7. The other team asked ____________ fans for support. (it's, its)

B. Circle the letter next to the correct definition of the underlined homograph.

8. Jason will run to the basket and <u>spring</u> into the air.

a. a season that follows winter **b.** to jump or leap

9. That tall, <u>lean</u> player is the best one on their team.

a. to stand slanting **b.** thin

10. We will meet at the west <u>entrance</u> to the field.

a. place to go in **b.** delight; charm

11. The coach is quite <u>stern</u> with the players.

a. strict **b.** back part of a ship

12. One <u>fan</u> hung up a huge banner.

a. a device for stirring the air **b.** an admirer

Extension: Have students write sentences using the two definitions of the following homographs: *hide, close,* and *loaf.* Then have them write a sentence using both meanings of the homophones *sight* and *site.*

Name ____________________

Grammar and Writing Connection: Combining Sentences

You can combine sentences by using *who, which,* or *that* to add details from one sentence to another.
When you add details that give essential information, use these words without commas.

Separate: Florence Nightingale was a famous English nurse. She helped establish modern methods for nursing.
Combined: Florence Nightingale was a famous English nurse who helped establish modern methods for nursing.

When you add details that give information that is not really essential, use *who* or *which* and put commas before and after the details.

Separate: Nightingale was born in Florence, Italy. She was the daughter of wealthy English parents.
Combined: Nightingale, who was the daughter of wealthy English parents, was born in Florence, Italy.

Combine each pair of sentences using *who, which,* or *that.* Add commas where they are needed.

1. Nightingale's father was a teacher. He helped her learn several languages as well as literature, art, and science.

____

____

2. Her family enrolled her in a "finishing" school. It was the normal type of education for a young English woman in the 1850s.

____

____

3. In 1851, at the age of 31, Nightingale began a career as a nurse. This was a highly unusual step for a woman of her time.

____

____

4. In 1854, she organized a unit of nurses for the Crimean War. This was going on in Central and Eastern Europe.

____

____

Extension: Have students write two pairs of sentences that can be combined using the words *which, who,* or *that.* Then have students exchange papers and combine the sentences. Remind them to use correct punctuation.

Name

Group Writing: A Biographical Sketch

A **biographical sketch** tells readers about the life and accomplishments of another person. A three-paragraph plan can be used for a biographical sketch.

Introduction: The introduction should contain facts, a quotation, or information about achievements or characteristics that will catch the reader's attention.

Body: The body tells the person's life story. It should be organized in chronological order.

Conclusion: The conclusion should tell something significant about the person's life. It can sum up the person's accomplishments, or personality, or both.

Read this part of a biographical sketch. Then answer the questions that follow.

"Alice," says her mother, Mrs. Dorothy Ward, "was always on the move. She was always doing five different things at once. Maybe that's why she got so far."

Alice Ward, of course, did go far. At the age of nineteen, while still in college, she began providing advice to local businesses about their computer systems. By the time she was twenty-one, she was head of a multi-million dollar computer empire. How did she do it? "I guess my secret was knowing what I was good at," she says. "I knew what my strength was—showing people how to get the most out of themselves, their equipment, even their employees. It was just nice to discover that people were willing to pay me a lot of money to show them how."

In a surprising move, Ward sold her business at the age of twenty-five, using the money to start a community service project that helps the unemployed find new jobs and careers. "I'm still in the same line of work," she says. "Only now, I don't worry about making money for myself. I just worry about helping other people."

1. Who is the subject of this biographical sketch? ______________________

2. What has this person accomplished? ______________________

____

3. In what order are the events of the person's life told? ______________________

4. How did the writer begin the biographical sketch? Circle one.

a. with an important event **b.** with a quotation **c.** with a characteristic

5. What does the last paragraph tell you about the person? ______________________

____

Extension: Have students write a short biographical sketch about a person they admire.

Name ______________________________

Thinking and Writing: Understanding Sequence

The body of a biographical sketch tells the story of the subject's life. The events that are included should be the most important ones in the person's life or ones that help readers understand the subject's character. The items or events should be arranged in **chronological order**, beginning with the subject's birth and childhood and concluding with the subject's death or, if the subject is still alive, with his or her present situation.

Read this page from a writer's notes for a biographical sketch of Emmeline Pankhurst. Then answer the questions that follow by writing the letters of the events on the lines.

a. In the summer of 1913, she left England for Paris.
b. Her actions forced British government to change some policies toward women.
c. Went on hunger strike in jail and was force-fed.
d. Her radical methods included breaking windows and setting fire to buildings and mailboxes.
e. Became an internationally famous figure.
f. Her violence turned many people away from women's rights movement.
g. Prison treatment damaged her health.
h. Pankhurst was an Englishwoman who worked for women's rights.
i. Released from prison because of her health.
j. Sent to jail in 1913.
k. Led first followers as they heckled speakers and marched in parades.
l. Brilliant and forceful woman.
m. Grew more radical after 1905.
n. Helped found Women's Franchise League, in 1889, and Women's Social and Political Union, in 1903.
o. Born in Manchester, England, in 1858.

1. Which details would you use in the introduction to this biographical sketch? ______________

2. Which of these details belong in the body of the sketch about Pankhurst?

____

3. In what order should the details be presented in the body of this biographical sketch?

____

4. Which details would you use in a conclusion to this biographical sketch? ______________

5. What additional information might you want to include in the biographical sketch?

____

____

Extension: Challenge students to find a biographical sketch in their reader or other school textbook. Then have them identify the author's purpose and plan for writing the sketch.

Name

Proofreading: Step 4

Indent ¶
Add ∧
Add a comma ∧,
Add quotation marks ∨ ∨
Add a period ⊙
Take out ℯ
Capitalize ≡
Make a small letter /
Reverse the order ∽

Read this paragraph about Jane Goodall. Check to see whether subject and object pronouns have been used correctly. Also, check to see whether apostrophes have been used where needed in contractions.

A. Mark corrections and additions in the paragraph with proofreading marks from the box.

Jane Goodall had been interested in animals from the time her was very young. Shed decided then that hers wanted to go to Africa and study they. Her did get to Africa, and hers met the anthropologist Dr. Louis Leakey there. Its turned out that him had a great influence on she. Him thought shed make a good field researcher. Her followed Leakey's advice, and her studied chimpanzee behavior for ten years. Shes written books and helped to make films about she experiences, and shes continuing her research still.

B. Write the paragraph correctly on the lines below. Make the corrections and additions you marked above.

Name

Adjectives

An **adjective** is a word that modifies or describes a noun or pronoun.

William Shakespeare wrote wonderful plays.

A **predicate adjective** is a word that describes a noun or pronoun in the subject. A predicate adjective must follow a linking verb.

His plays are both complex and entertaining.

Present and past participles are often used as adjectives or predicate adjectives.

Those much-loved plays are exciting.

Underline each adjective once, and underline each predicate adjective twice. Then draw an arrow from that adjective to the noun or pronoun that it describes.

1. The great playwright William Shakespeare was born in tiny Stratford-on-Avon, England, in 1564.
2. Shakespeare's background and education were typical for children of the time.
3. Little is known of this marvelous writer's early years.
4. He probably traveled to bustling London around 1590 and joined one of many acting companies in the capital.
5. London was filled with brilliant poets and exciting dramatists.
6. From 1594 to 1608, Shakespeare concentrated his writing talent on London's busy theaters.
7. He quickly became famous for both his tragedies and his comedies.
8. Shakespeare grew both popular and wealthy from his work.
9. People would fill crowded theaters to see plays by this noted and popular writer.
10. In 1599, Shakespeare and some associates took over their own theater just outside London.
11. Their theater became famous all over England.
12. Shakespeare's lengthy career reached its peak from 1599 to 1608.
13. Many of his great tragedies were published during this creative period of his life.

Extension: Have students write five sentences about a place they have visited. Have them use adjectives or predicate adjectives in each sentence.

Name

Articles and Proper Adjectives

The words *a, an,* and *the* are special adjectives called **articles.**
A and *an* are called **indefinite articles** because they refer to one of a general group of people, places, things, or ideas. *A* is used before words beginning with a consonant sound, while *an* is used before words beginning with a vowel sound.

a vacation   an adventure   a plane   an event

The is called a **definite article** because it identifies a specific person, place, thing, or idea.

the car   the boy   the ticket

A **proper adjective** is an adjective formed from a proper noun. A proper adjective is capitalized.

Mexican silver   Central American countries

On the lines below, rewrite each sentence that contains errors in the use of articles or proper adjectives. If a sentence contains no errors, circle the number of that sentence.

1. Jan's family is planning an caribbean vacation this year.

2. They will leave the airport early on Tuesday morning.

3. By early afternoon, they will be enjoying a puerto rican sunshine.

4. The family will spend an few days in Puerto Rico.

5. Jan's father and mother visited the Mexican coast several years ago.

6. This time they are spending a part of the time on island beaches.

7. The family will stay at a estate on the island of St. Thomas.

8. The estate is owned by a south american friend of Jan's father.

Extension: Have students write six sentences about what they saw when they went on a class outing or field trip. Have them use a proper adjective and a definite or indefinite article in each sentence.

Name ______________________________

Comparative and Superlative Adjectives I

The **comparative** form of an adjective compares two people or things. The comparative of most adjectives is formed by adding *er*.

Josh is older than Will.

The **superlative** form of an adjective compares more than two people or things. The superlative of most adjectives is formed by adding *est*.

Josh is the oldest child in his family.

Some adjectives are **irregular** and do not form the comparative and superlative by adding *er* or *est*.

good → better → best   bad → worse → worst

A. Complete each sentence with the correct form of the adjective in parentheses.

1. The Florida Everglades is one of the ______________ swamps in the world. (large)
2. Few places in the world are ______________ than this exotic swamp. (strange)
3. Junglelike foliage and intricate waterways make it one of the ______________ places in the world to explore. (hard)
4. Many of the plants in the Everglades area grow ______________ there than anywhere else. (big)
5. Mangrove trees, for example, seldom grow ______________ than the seventy-foot giants of the Everglades. (tall)
6. Some of the ______________ flowers in the world grow wild in this fertile area. (lovely)
7. The ______________ of all are perhaps the wild orchids. (pretty)
8. There also are ______________ crocodiles, alligators, and giant turtles there than almost anywhere else in North America. (many)

B. Fill in the missing forms of the adjectives listed on the chart below.

Adjective	Comparative Form	Superlative Form
		warmest
	worse	
much		
	harder	

Extension: Have students identify each adjective in Part A by writing **C** for *comparative* or **S** for *superlative*.

Name ______________________________

Comparative and Superlative Adjectives II

Remember these rules for forming the comparative and superlative forms of adjectives.

- Add *er* or *est* to most one-syllable adjectives.

  fast → faster → fastest

- If an adjective has two syllables, add *er* or *est*, or use the words *more* and *most* or *less* and *least.*

  happy → happier → happiest
  fruitful → more fruitful → most fruitful

- If an adjective has three or more syllables, do not add *er* or *est.* Instead, use the words *more* and *most* or *less* and *least.*

  serious → less serious → least serious

- Do not use *more* and *most* or *less* and *least* before comparative or superlative adjectives ending in *er* or *est.*

Complete each sentence with the correct form of the adjective in parentheses. Remember to add *er* or *est, more* or *most,* or *less* or *least* to form the comparative and superlative.

1. The Clayton School's Spring Concert is the ______________________ event of the year. (popular)

2. Each year the program seems ______________________ than the last. (thrilling)

3. The members of the band, orchestra, and chorus put on their ______________________ performances. (good)

4. The band program is one of the ______________________ parts of the concert. (lively)

5. The band plays ______________________ music like marches, show tunes, and movie themes. (exciting)

6. The orchestra generally plays ______________________ fare. (sophisticated)

7. This year, however, it will play some movie themes that are ______________________ than its usual fare. (well known)

8. The audience's ______________________ response is always reserved for the school chorus. (enthusiastic)

9. The chorus always sings some of the year's ______________________ hits. (great)

10. Everyone hopes that this year's concert will be ______________________ than any other. (successful)

Extension: Have students write six sentences, leaving a blank where an adjective of comparison should be. Then have students exchange papers, fill in the correct adjective, and identify it as comparative or superlative.

PRACTICE-60

Name

Demonstrative Adjectives

This, that, these, and *those* are used to point out items that are far away. *This, that, these,* and *those* are **demonstrative adjectives** when they describe nouns. They answer the questions *which one?* or *which ones?*

We will climb that mountain.

Demonstrative pronouns also point out something. They take the place of nouns.

That is a difficult peak to scale.

Do not use *here* or *there* when using a demonstrative adjective. Do not use the object pronoun *them* in place of the demonstrative adjective *those.*

On the lines below, correct any errors in the use of demonstrative adjectives by writing the sentences correctly. Circle the number in front of any sentence that is correct.

1. This snow-covered mountain in the distance is Mount Columbia.
2. These peaks over there are part of the Rocky Mountain chain.
3. The Tetons are among the most spectacular mountains in this area.
4. This road is about twenty miles away and leads directly into Rocky Mountain National Park.
5. Deer, elk, and bighorn sheep all make their homes in that park.
6. Lewis and Clark and Zebulon Pike were among the first American explorers of those there mountains.
7. That trail we are on leads up into the mountains.
8. Our guide will take us right up the trail and into them mountains.
9. This compass on my wrist is very useful for hiking and climbing.
10. We will camp for the night right in this here clearing.

Extension: Have students look through a magazine or newspaper article and find five sentences containing demonstrative adjectives. Then have them identify the word each demonstrative adjective modifies.

Name

Adverbs

An **adverb** is a word that modifies, or tells more about a verb, an adjective or another adverb. Adverbs usually answer the question *how? when? where?* or *to what extent?*

How: The torch carrier ran past the loudly (Adverb) cheering (Adjective) crowd.

When: Today (Adverb) he ran (Verb) with the Olympic Torch.

Where: He ran (Verb) forward (Adverb).

To What Extent: He ran very (Adverb) quickly (Adverb).

Underline each adverb in the sentences below. Then draw an arrow to the word it modifies.

1. The Olympic Games open spectacularly with a special ceremony.
2. Before the beginning of the games, extremely dedicated runners make a long journey.
3. The journey begins in Olympia, Greece, the valley in which the very first Olympic Games were held.
4. At Olympia, a torch is first lit from a flame that symbolizes the Olympic spirit.
5. A runner quickly departs, carrying the torch towards the site of this year's games.
6. This torch now will link the next Olympic Games to the entire Olympic tradition.
7. The runners proudly carry the torch over an established route.
8. Each runner covers a given distance before carefully passing the torch to another runner.
9. Swiftly, the torch makes its way from one country to another.
10. Ships and planes transport the brightly burning flame across impassable mountains or bodies of water.
11. The torch soon reaches the site of the present Olympic Games.
12. In the opening ceremonies, the Olympic flame is dramatically lighted from this burning torch from Greece.

Extension: Have students write six sentences about an Olympic event they have read about or seen on television. Have them use adverbs in every sentence.

Name ______________________________

Comparative and Superlative Adverbs

The **comparative** form of an adverb is used to compare two actions. The **superlative** form of an adverb is used to compare more than two actions.

- Add *er* or *est* to form the comparative or superlative of most one-syllable adverbs and some adverbs with more than one syllable.

  late → later → latest

- Use *more* or *most* to form the comparative and superlative of some two-syllable adverbs and all adverbs with more than two syllables.

  peacefully → more peacefully → most peacefully

- Use *less* and *least* to form negative comparisons.

  less high   least high

- Do not use *more* and *most* or *less* and *least* with adverbs that already have *er* or *est* added to them.
- Remember that some adverbs have irregular comparative and superlative forms.

  badly → worse → worst

Complete each sentence by writing the correct form of the adverb in parentheses.

1. The storm approached ______________________ than any we had ever seen before. (quickly)

2. Luckily, the people of the town prepared ______________________ for this storm than for the last hurricane. (well)

3. People waited ______________________ by their televisions and radios for news of the storm. (eagerly)

4. The storm, however, arrived ______________________ than people had anticipated. (soon)

5. Winds struck ______________________ than anyone had ever experienced before. (powerfully)

6. Officials steered people away from the roads traveled ______________________. (frequently)

7. The waterfront area was the ______________________ damaged of all by the storm. (seriously)

8. Each wave struck the dock ______________________ than the one before. (furiously)

Extension: Have students write six sentences, leaving blanks where the adverb should be. Then have students exchange papers, fill in the correct adverb, and identify its degree of comparison.

PRACTICE-63

Name ____________________

Avoiding Double Negatives

A **double negative** is the incorrect use of two negative words to convey a negative meaning.

Joan and Jacki hadn't never been camping before.

There are two ways you can correct a sentence with a double negative. The first way is to eliminate one of the negative words.

Joan and Jacki had never been camping before.
Joan and Jacki hadn't been camping before.

The second way is to replace one of the negative words with its positive form.

Joan and Jacki hadn't ever been camping before.

Complete each sentence using the correct word in parentheses.

1. Hardly ____________________ was going right for the two girls as they prepared for their first camping trip. (anything, nothing)
2. It was almost noon, but the two girls still had not gotten ____________________ of their gear packed. (any, none)
3. "Nobody should go ____________________ without planning ahead," Joan said, frustrated. (anywhere, nowhere)
4. When they finally got on their way, though, they had hardly ____________________ problems. (any, no)
5. They ____________________ been on the trail for hardly an hour or two when they came upon a small valley. (had, hadn't)
6. The girls hadn't ____________________ seen anything quite as beautiful. (ever, never)
7. There weren't flowers or trees like these ____________________ else the girls had ever been. (anywhere, nowhere)
8. It seemed as if no one else ____________________ came to the lovely valley. (ever, never)
9. In fact, Jacki didn't think that ____________________ had ever been in this secluded part of the country. (anybody, nobody)
10. "Promise that you ____________________ never tell anyone about this secret place," she demanded to Joan. (will, won't)

Extension: Have students write five sentences containing double negatives. Then have students exchange papers and rewrite the sentences, correcting the double negatives.

PRACTICE-64

Name ________________________________

Using Adjectives and Adverbs

An **adjective** is a word that modifies, or describes, a noun or pronoun.
An **adverb** is a word that modifies, or tells more about, a verb, an adjective or another adverb.
Many adverbs are formed by adding *ly* to an adjective.

Adjective	Adverb	Adjective	Adverb
patient →	patiently	helpful →	helpfully

Do not confuse these adjectives and adverbs:

Adjectives	Adverbs
real	really
bad	badly
good	well

Complete each sentence by writing the correct word in parentheses. Then draw an arrow from that word to the word that it modifies.

1. This autumn, Carla's family took a ____________________ trip to New York City. (wonderful, wonderfully)
2. They arrived on a Thursday morning and unpacked their things ____________________. (quick, quickly)
3. Carla ____________________ wanted to see as much as she could. (real, really)
4. That afternoon they had a ____________________ time just walking around the crowded city streets. (good, well)
5. Carla's mother and father enjoyed seeing all the ____________________ decorated stores and shops. (bright, brightly)
6. That evening, they dressed up and went to a ____________________ restaurant for dinner. (fancy, fancily)
7. Carla's brother ate so much that, later that evening, he did not feel ____________________. (good, well)
8. The next day they ____________________ made their way through the Museum of Natural History, the Museum of Modern Art, and the Museum of the American Indian. (happy, happily)
9. By the end of the day, they ____________________ returned to their hotel rooms for a rest! (glad, gladly)

Extension: Have students write five sentences, leaving blanks where the adverb or adjective should be. Then have students exchange papers, fill in the correct modifier, and tell whether it is an adjective or adverb.

Name

Mechanics: Commas with Dates, Addresses, and Names

- Use commas before and after the year when it is used with both the month and the day. Do not use a comma if you use only the month and year.

  Mary Flynn became a nurse on June 30, 1966. She began work in August 1966.

- Use commas before and after the name of a state or country when it is used with the name of a city.

  Mercy Hospital is in Durham, North Carolina, in the north end of town.

- Use a comma or a pair of commas to set off an abbreviated title or degree following a person's name.

  Mary Flynn, R.N., works at Mercy Hospital.

- Use a comma after the salutation of a friendly letter and after the closing of both a friendly and a business letter.

  Dear Thomas, Your friend, Sincerely yours,

Add commas wherever needed in the following letter.

456 Simpson Drive
Rawlings Illinois 21390
July 6 1990

Bernice Jonas M.D.
32 Eagle Drive
Boston Massachusetts 10021

Dear Bernice

It's great to hear that you are now a doctor, and I am sorry that I could not get to Boston Massachusetts to see your graduation. But, on June 12 1990 our whole family was in Hawaii. As you can see from these pictures, we stayed in Honolulu Hawaii at a wonderful hotel. We enjoyed sunshine, warm weather, and, best of all, a lot of swimming. A friend of my father's, Randy Fillmore Ph.D. even started to show me how to surf. On our way back home we stopped in San Francisco California for a few days. We had a great time seeing all the sights. We even took a drive up to Seattle Washington to see my cousin Eleanor. Now that I'm back, please write to me as soon as you can.

Your friend
Carla

Extension: Have students work with a partner to explain why commas were added to the letter on this page.

Name

Vocabulary Building: Synonyms and Antonyms

A **synonym** is a word that has the same or nearly the same meaning as another word. You can use synonyms to be more descriptive and precise in your writing.

Marion skates easily. Marion skates gracefully.

An **antonym** is a word that means the opposite of another word. You can use antonyms to contrast ideas in your writing.

Chris skated poorly at first, but soon did very well.

Rewrite each sentence, using first a synonym and then an antonym for each underlined word.

1. Mark found a small bird beneath the big tree in the backyard.

2. He quickly picked up the bird and brought it inside.

3. His brother was not pleased with the idea of caring for the bird, and he reluctantly agreed to help.

4. After a few days, the bird seemed to improve.

5. Mark was determined to help the bird, and after a short while the bird slowly began to recover.

Extension: Challenge students to form teams and see which team can list the most synonyms for each of the following words in five minutes: *quickly*, *small*, and *new*. Then have students supply an antonym for each.

Name

Grammar and Writing Connection: Combining Sentences

Combining sentences can help you avoid repeating unnecessary words in your writing.
One way to combine sentences is to use words ending in *ing* or *ed*.
Sometimes the word ending in *ing* or *ed* is part of a group of words.

Separate: The fans cheered the runners. The runners were speeding past the grandstand.
Combined: The fans cheered the runners speeding past the grandstand.

These words can also be used alone.

Separate: The runners approached the finish line. They were exhausted.
Combined: The exhausted runners approached the finish line.

Combine each pair of sentences using words that end in *ed* or *ing*.

1. Ellen wrote a report. She was describing the history of the Olympic Games.

2. The ancient Greeks kept lists of great athletes. The athletes were honored for their victories in the Olympic Games.

3. The athletes competed in foot races and other contests. The contests were honoring the chief god of the ancient Greeks.

4. The spectators cheered their favorites. The spectators were excited.

5. Other events were added to the games. The games were loved by the Greek people.

Extension: Have students write three pairs of separate sentences that can be combined by using words ending in *ing* or *ed*. Then have students exchange papers and combine the sentences.

Name

Group Writing: A Description

The purpose of **descriptive writing** is to give a clear and vivid picture of a person, place, or thing. An effective description has three elements:

- An **overall impression** that is the general idea to be given to the reader.
- **Sensory details** that appeal to one or more of the reader's senses—sight, hearing, touch, taste, or smell.
- An **ordering of details** that follows a logical plan. They may be ordered according to each particular sense, according to order of importance, or even from front-to-back or from back-to-front.

Read the descriptive paragraph. Then answer the questions that follow.

The ballpark was crowded, filled with the murmur of thousands of people waiting expectantly. The smells of popcorn and hot dogs drifted through the stadium. All the seats were filled, and fans lined the back walls of the old gray and blue building. Down below on the playing field, the players could be seen: tiny dots of white and red or gray and green. Seen from the very last rows of the bleachers, the teams resembled tiny dots moving about in a computer game. But, from the expensive seats along the base lines, the dots became real people striving to do their best in the contest to come. And, throughout the entire stadium, the cries of the vendors drifted, like the calls of giant birds: "Peeeeeeanutsssss! Hot dooooggs! Coooold drrrriiinks!" The voices made people as hungry for food as they were for the spectacle of the World Series that was about to begin.

1. What is this paragraph about? ______________________________

____

2. What overall impression does the paragraph give? ______________________________

____

3. What senses does the paragraph appeal to? ______________________________

4. What sense(s) does the paragraph *not* appeal to? ______________________________

5. What details in the paragraph appeal to the senses? ______________________________

____

Extension: Have students write a short description of a place or object using figurative language.

Name

Thinking and Writing: Classifying

Classifying is giving a name to a group of things and emphasizing a feature they have in common. In writing, classifying often is used to group sensory details together for a descriptive paragraph. Making a chart that classifies the details according to the five senses—sight, hearing, touch, taste, and smell, is an effective way of organizing your thinking.

As you read the paragraph, look for sensory details that help you see a vivid picture of the house and yard. Then, write the appropriate details under each of the groups.

The house loomed above us, gray and black, looking almost like a giant mountain at the end of the street. Over the years, the house had fallen into such disrepair that, in many parts of the building, there seemed to be nothing left but the faded paint. Shutters hung from a single hinge and creaked . . . creaked . . . creaked in the breeze. The glass from broken windows littered the yard and front walk, so that every step had a crunching sound—and an unpleasant feel. The yard also was home to an old swing that moved gently back and forth in the wind, its ropes making a thunk . . . thunk each time it moved. Off to the side, a gazebo, a small round building with open sides, reminded us of how busy and beautiful the house once had been. Then, we smelled musty clothes and old furniture—as if an old trunk had been opened after many years. Someone must have left some old things outside a long time ago.

Sights

Sounds

Feel

Smells

Extension: Have students list sensory details they might encounter during a visit to the library. Have them classify the details under the headings: Sights, Sounds, Smells, Feel.

PRACTICE-70

Name

Proofreading: Step 4

Indent ¶
Add ∧
Add a comma ∧,
Add quotation marks ∨ ∨
Add a period ⊙
Take out
Capitalize ≡
Make a small letter /
Reverse the order ∽

Read the paragraph about the ancient Phoenicians. See whether adjectives and adverbs are used correctly. Also, see whether all proper adjectives are capitalized.

A. Use the proofreading marks from the box to mark any corrections in the paragraph.

In ancient times, the Phoenicians lived on a narrowly strip of coast along the Mediterranean Sea. Their interests turned natural to seafaring because their land was dryly and hilly. These people quick became adventurously sailors. They enthusiastic explored the sea and eventual established severally colonies, some on mediterranean islands. As they traveled wide, the phoenician sailors also spread their culture to variously lands. The greek alphabet, as a matter of fact, was actual adapted from one original developed by the Phoenicians.

B. Use the corrections you marked above to write the paragraph correctly on the lines below.

Name

Prepositions and Prepositional Phrases

A **preposition** is a word that shows a relationship between a noun or a pronoun and another word in a sentence.

The new book is on the shelf.

A **prepositional phrase** is a group of words that begins with a preposition and ends with a noun or a pronoun. The noun or pronoun that follows the preposition is called the **object of the preposition.**

Preposition **Object of Preposition**

Randy took the book to her desk.

Prepositional Phrase

Circle each prepositional phrase. Underline the preposition once and the object of the preposition twice.

1. Carrie told us about several new books.
2. She found one book among her mother's old college books.
3. It was a textbook for a journalism course.
4. She got another book from the library.
5. This book described life at a major metropolitan newspaper.
6. Carrie was fascinated by it.
7. She now wants to learn more about journalism.
8. Our friend Lara found a book about community organizations.
9. It describes organizations for many civic purposes.
10. She explained them to us.
11. Mark wants a book on community planning.
12. He has searched through many libraries.
13. We hope he finally finds something within the next few weeks.
14. We are planning a new swimming facility for our town.
15. A book about community projects would be very helpful.
16. The new pool would go behind the playing fields.

Extension: Have students write five sentences containing prepositional phrases. Then have them underline the object of the preposition in each.

Name ______________________________

Using Pronouns in Prepositional Phrases

When a pronoun is used as the object of the preposition, the object form of the pronoun is used.

I loaned the book to him.

If a preposition has two or more words as its object, they are called a **compound object.** Always use object pronouns in a compound object.

Compound Object

We bought the book for Jana and her.

When the word *me* is used in a compound object of a preposition, make sure that it always comes last.

The librarian saved that book for Sarah and me.

Do not use a reflexive pronoun when an object pronoun will convey your meaning.

Jason went to the library with Fran and ~~myself~~. ← me

A. Write the pronoun you could use in place of the underlined word or words in each sentence.

1. ______________ Have you read that book about forest rangers?
2. ______________ Everyone has read it except Paul and Maria.
3. ______________ Terry will loan it to Carrie and (your name).
4. ______________ I placed another interesting book between Carrie and me.
5. ______________ We could not have read the book without Nick.

B. On the lines below, rewrite any sentences in which the pronouns are not used correctly. Circle the number next to any sentence that is correct.

6. Several of we went to the library this afternoon.
7. We waited in the library quite a while for him.
8. Sarah showed a wonderful book to me and Tim.
9. The book on sailboats seemed especially written for Ben and myself.
10. It seemed unusually quiet in the reading room to Cara and I.

____

____

____

____

Extension: Challenge students to write four more example sentences for Part B. Have them exchange papers and write the correct pronoun, if needed, for each sentence.

Name ______________________________

Prepositional Phrases as Adjectives or Adverbs

An **adjective phrase** is a prepositional phrase that functions as an adjective.

The gym in our school is quite small.

An **adverb phrase** is a prepositional phrase that functions as an adverb.

Verb **Adverb Phrase**

Students play in the gym almost every day.

Adjective **Adverb Phrase**

The gym has been inadequate for several years.

Adverb **Adverb Phrase**

People run cautiously under the leaky roof.

A. Write the prepositional phrase in each sentence. Then write whether it is an **adjective** or an **adverb** phrase.

1. People from many companies have visited the gym. ______________________________
2. A new gym will be built in the spring. ______________________________
3. Everyone has thought carefully about the plans. ______________________________
4. For many reasons, the new gym seems wonderful. ______________________________
5. Basketball can be played on three different courts. ______________________________

B. Underline each prepositional phrase once. Underline the word it modifies twice.

6. Equipment for gymnastics also has been obtained.
7. A swimming pool will be installed under the gym.
8. A swimming team for students will be organized soon.
9. School officials are cautious about future plans.
10. One announcement from the office had detailed drawings.
11. Officials in charge have tight budget restrictions.
12. Some plans will be approved at the school board's next meeting.
13. A few decisions about the matter have been postponed.
14. Most students are happy about the plans.
15. In the meantime, they wait anxiously.

Extension: Have students write **adjective** or **adverb** to describe the function of each prepositional phrase in Part B.

Name ____________________

Using Verbs After Prepositional Phrases

When a prepositional phrase comes between the subject and verb of a sentence, make sure that the verb agrees with the subject of the sentence, and not with the object of the preposition.

Plural Subject **Object of Preposition**

Communities around the country are concerned with the environment.

Plural Verb

One way to make sure the subject and verb do agree is to "cross out" the prepositional phrase. That way you can see the subject and verb more clearly.

Communities ~~around the country~~ favor recycling and other environmental measures.

A. Write the form of the verb in parentheses that will correctly complete the sentence.

1. ____________ Pollutants of many kinds (has, have) become a major problem.

2. ____________ Water in lakes and rivers (is, are) not usable.

3. ____________ Air from various sources (pollute, pollutes) many cities.

4. ____________ Industrial pollution of many varieties (affects, affect) communities in all parts of the country.

5. ____________ Emissions from an automobile or a truck also (cause, causes) breathing problems for many people.

B. Underline the subject of each sentence once. Underline the verb twice. If the subject and verb agree, write **correct** on the line beside the sentence. If they do not agree, write the correct form of the verb.

____________ **6.** People throughout the country is solving the problem.

____________ **7.** Laws of all kinds have been passed.

____________ **8.** Cars in this country is equipped with anti-pollution devices.

____________ **9.** Cities and industries under the new law limits emissions into the air.

____________ **10.** Inspectors from the government check on the situation.

____________ **11.** A factory near rivers or lakes now limit pollution.

____________ **12.** Many rivers in our country are the cleanest they have been in almost a century.

Extension: Have students underline the subjects of the sentences in Part A once and the verbs twice. Then have students write whether the subject and verb are singular or plural.

Name ______________________________

Conjunctions

Conjunctions connect parts of sentences. A **coordinating conjunction** is one word used to connect the different parts of a sentence or to connect two sentences. *And, but, or, for,* and *nor* are common coordinating conjunctions.

Compound Subject: Radio and television reach millions of people.
Compound Predicate: The shows relax and amuse them.
Compound Sentence: Television was difficult to develop, and many people contributed to the effort.

Notice that a comma is used before a coordinating conjuction that joins two sentences. A **correlative conjunction** is a pair of words used to connect the parts of a sentence. *Both . . . and, either . . . or, neither . . . nor, not only . . . but also, whether . . . or, just as . . . so,* are common correlative conjunctions.

Neither its inventors nor early broadcasters foresaw TV's great success.

Write each conjunction and then label it **coordinating** or **correlative**.

______________ **1.** A working but imperfect television system was demonstrated
______________ as early as 1929.

______________ **2.** In 1936, the Radio Corporation of America installed 150
______________ television sets in New York City and its suburbs.

______________ **3.** Just as the transmissions were experimental, so were the
______________ early shows that were broadcast.

______________ **4.** Both entertainment and news programs were broadcast.

______________ **5.** After World War II, national networks began television
______________ broadcasts, and the "TV boom" began.

______________ **6.** Not only news and sports but also variety shows were
______________ transmitted into American homes each day.

______________ **7.** Almost everyone in America wanted a TV set, and the
______________ number of sets grew from 10,000, in 1945, to almost 60
million, in 1960.

______________ **8.** Television meant great stardom for Milton Berle and
______________ Lucille Ball.

Extension: Have students write six sentences, three joined by a coordinating conjunction and three joined by a correlative conjunction.

Name

Making Verbs Agree with Compound Subjects

A **compound subject** contains two or more simple subjects joined by a conjuction. When two or more subjects are joined by *and* or *both . . . and*, the verb is plural.

Both Mickey and Roberto favor year-round school.
Jana and Lucy are not quite sure.

When two or more subjects are joined by *or*, *nor*, *either . . . or*, or *neither . . . nor*, the verb agrees with the subject that is closest to it.

Instruction or tests occur all year long.

Underline the correct form of the verb in parentheses and circle the simple subjects in each sentence.

1. Today, most elementary-school children and high-school students (attend, attends) classes ten months of the year.
2. Neither long vacations nor individual holidays (is, are) counted in this total.
3. Today, however, some teachers and officials (want, wants) an increase in this time.
4. (Do, Does) both students and teachers benefit from this?
5. Grades and attitude often (improve, improves) a great deal.
6. Either several short vacations or one long break (is, are) needed, according to some educators.
7. According to others, however, a shorter vacation or no vacation (promote, promotes) learning.
8. Neither students nor teachers (seem, seems) upset by a shorter vacation.
9. One-day national holidays and long weekends (give, gives) time off scattered throughout the year.
10. Neither farm chores nor the harvest (require, requires) students' labor throughout the summer.
11. Many children and their parents (take, takes) a family trip during July or August.
12. Either several weeks or one week (is, are) the time most parents can take for trips.
13. Perhaps both the teachers and the other school employees (need, needs) a rest from classes.
14. Teachers and parents (disagree, disagrees) on the proposals.

Extension: Have students write six sentences joined by a compound subject, leaving a blank where the verb should be. Then have students exchange papers and fill in the correct form of the verb.

Name ______________________________

Interjections

An **interjection** is a word or phrase used to express strong feeling. Here are some common interjections.

Ah!	Good heavens!	Hey!	Phew!	Oops!
Gee!	Goodness!	Oh, my!	Yippee!	Whoopee!
Golly!	Gosh!	Oh, no!	Hooray!	Wow!

An interjection can stand alone, followed by an exclamation mark, or it can begin a sentence, followed by a comma. An interjection that stands alone usually expresses a stronger feeling than an interjection that is used as part of a sentence.

Goodness, what a large group of people.
Wow! What a speech!

Underline the interjection in each sentence. Then add the correct punctuation.

1. Gosh I've never been to a political convention before.
2. People are crowding in all over. Wow
3. Hey Isn't that my favorite actor over there?
4. Oops You stepped on my foot!
5. Gosh did you see that?
6. Golly it's all so exciting.
7. I can't see now. Yikes
8. Yeah Here they come!
9. Hey Start cheering!
10. Yippee We won.
11. Hey Here comes the candidate!
12. Listen to the band play! Wow
13. Gee it all seems quite a big show, doesn't it?
14. Good heavens do you think this candidate will win?
15. Oh, my can I sing along, too?
16. Wow What a cheer.
17. Oh, my my voice is getting hoarse.
18. Oh, no my voice is completely gone.
19. Well my hands can still applaud.
20. Ah that's what I'll do.

Extension: Have students work in pairs to write a dialogue in which each sentence contains an interjection.

PRACTICE-78

Name

Mechanics: Using Semicolons and Colons

A **semicolon** is used to join parts of a compound sentence when a coordinating conjunction is not used.

The rally will begin at 10:15; the topic is anti-pollution legislation.

A semicolon is also used to join the parts of a compound sentence when commas are already used to subdivide independent clauses.

Speakers will discuss pollution, answer questions, and present proposals; and a large assembly is expected.

A colon is used to introduce a list of items that ends a sentence. A phrase such as *the following* or *as follows* should come before the list.

The following speakers are expected: Dr. Bob Duffy, Juan Perez, and Mayor Farrell.

A colon is also used to separate the hour and minute when you write the time of day, and after the salutation of a business letter.

10:30 Dear Senator Lowell:

Add colons and semicolons where they are needed in the following letter.

45 Macon Drive
Middleton, Ohio 43210
November 15, 1990

Senator William Bell
Senate Office Building
Washington, D.C. 20510

Dear Senator Bell

Our group, the Citizens Against Environmental Pollution, is holding a rally to demonstrate our support for anti-pollution legislation. We would appreciate it if you could attend and speak to the assembled group. The rally, which will begin at 1015 A.M. on Thursday, December 1, is expected to attract many political figures, including the governor and the mayor several celebrities who are active in the anti-pollution drive and community leaders. The following other groups have announced their participation in the effort the Ohio Anti-Pollution League, the Save the Earth Fund, and the Middleton Civic Association. Each group will send speakers to the rally we anticipate participation from other groups as well. The rally has been organized carefully in fact, it is expected to be one of the most successful efforts of its kind ever held. We look forward to an appearance by you please advise us of your interest.

Sincerely,

A. Wilson Duncan, President

Extension: Have students write a short business letter to the mayor of their town or other elected representative, discussing a recycling plan that they would like to see implemented. Have them use colons and semicolons.

Name ______

PRACTICE-79

Vocabulary Building: Prefixes

A **prefix** is a word part added to the beginning of a base word. A prefix changes the meaning of the base word to which it is added.
Here are some common prefixes and their meanings.

Prefix	Meaning	Example
bi	two	bimonthly
inter	between	intercity
post	after	postwar
pre	before	predawn
re	again, back	retell
sub	under, lower	submarine
in, il, im, ir	without, not	inexpensive
mis	wrongly	misspell
non	not	nonsense

A. Underline the prefix in each word. Then use the prefix and root word to figure out its meaning. Write the meaning of the word.

1. misguide ______

2. biplane ______

3. nonsense ______

4. subzero ______

5. interrupt ______

6. improper ______

7. unicycle ______

8. postwar ______

9. intersession ______

10. preheat ______

B. Complete each sentence by writing a prefixed word that means the same as the word or words in parentheses.

11. Flying the plane without a license was ______. (not legal)

12. It would be ______ to do that. (not responsible)

13. The mechanics would have to ______ the plane's battery before the engine would start. (charge again)

14. Marcia's parents do not ______ of her flying lessons. (not approve)

15. We stared in ______ as Marcia's plane took to the air. (not believing)

16. In the ______ excitement, Marcia forgot to remove her flying helmet. (after the flight)

Extension: Have students use five of the words defined in Part A in sentences.

Name

Grammar and Writing Connection: Combining Sentences

Combining sentences can make your writing more varied and interesting. When you combine sentences, avoid repeating words.
You can use prepositional phrases to combine sentences.

Separate: Mammoth Cave is one of the most popular places in North America. It is located in central Kentucky.
Combined: Mammoth Cave in central Kentucky is one of the most popular places in North America.

The objects of the prepositional phrase may be compound.

Separate: Tourists visit many areas.
Some areas are in the cave.
Other areas are in the park.
Combined: Tourists visit many areas in the cave and the park.

You may also combine sentences by moving adjectives from one sentence to another.

Separate: Visitors examine the cave.
They look at rock formations.
The formations are wonderful.
Combined: Visitors examine the wonderful rock formations inside the cave.

Combine each group of sentences by using prepositional phrases and adjectives.

1. A hunter named Robert Houchins discovered Mammoth Cave. He found it during a bear hunt.

2. The cave became famous. It became famous in the War of 1812. It became well known for its valuable mineral deposits.

3. Mining stopped after the war. It stopped soon.

4. The park became a showplace. It was for spectators. They were fascinated.

5. Since then, people have gone through the cave many times. They also have traveled down its passageways.

Extension: Have students write three pairs of separate sentences that can be joined by using prepositional phrases. Then have students exchange papers and combine the sentences.

Name

Group Writing: An Editorial

An **editorial** is a kind of persuasive writing that appears in a newspaper or magazine. The purpose of an editorial is to persuade an audience to think or act in a certain way. The topic sentence at the beginning of an editorial states an **opinion.** The remainder of the editorial presents **facts** arranged in **order of importance** that support the opinion. An editorial concludes with a **sentence that restates** the opinion or sums up the reasons for supporting it.

Read the following editorial and answer the questions about it.

Marcie Blaine is the best candidate for student council president of the Brandon River Middle School. Most important, Marcie Blaine has already served on the student council for two years. This makes her one of the most experienced members of that group. Marcie Blaine also has shown herself to be a highly creative person, and her ideas have helped this school in many ways. Her proposal for a new bus schedule helped eliminate the overcrowding that made bus rides unbearable for many students. Her idea for the Fall Blast turned out to be the school's most successful social event of the year. And, her ability to get along with both the faculty and administration of this school has helped her secure their support for many different clubs and projects. More than any other candidate, Marcie Blaine has proved herself able—and willing—to make this a better school for all students.

1. What is the topic of this editorial? __________

2. What is the writer's opinion? __________

3. What reasons does the writer give to support the opinion?

4. Which reason does the writer consider most important? __________

5. What does the concluding sentence tell you? __________

Extension: Have students cut out an editorial from a newspaper. Then have them identify its topic sentence, opinion, and the facts or reasons that support the opinion.

Name

Thinking and Writing: Faulty Methods of Persuasion

Persuasive writing tries to convince someone to accept an opinion. Valid persuasive writing presents fair and honest reasons supporting that opinion. Faulty persuasive writing often uses one or more of these invalid methods of persuasion:

- **Slanted facts:** These present only one side of an issue.
- **Charged words:** These are words that appeal to the emotions and make something sound better or worse than it really is.
- **Bandwagon:** This tells readers that everyone is doing or supporting something, so that they should do it, too.
- **Either-or thinking:** This tells readers that there are only two choices, when there may be many.

Label each statement **slanted facts, charged words, bandwagon,** or **either-or thinking**.

1. Margot Chambers has been a great student council officer. She is hard-working, creative, and interested in making this a wonderful school for everyone. Vote for her in this week's council election.

   ____

2. Everyone is supporting Jason Ruiz for mayor. Are you?

   ____

3. Randy is too uptight to be a student council president.

   ____

4. Either we start a school radio station or we will miss our last chance at having a wonderful activity for our school.

   ____

5. Motorboats are ruining Langdon Pond. They pollute the water. They make too much noise. They make it impossible to swim peacefully. Ban them from our pond.

   ____

6. If this community doesn't build a new recreation center, serious problems will develop.

   ____

7. Don't be the one person in town to oppose the new school building.

   ____

Extension: Have students find examples of the persuasive writing described on this page as well as other methods of persuasion in newspapers and magazines. Have them work together to make a bulletin board displaying the methods.

Name

Proofreading: Step 4

Indent ¶
Add ∧
Add a comma ∧,
Add quotation marks ∨ ∨
Add a period ⊙
Take out
Capitalize ≡
Make a small letter /
Reverse the order

Read this paragraph about plans for a seventh-grade class car wash. Check to see whether subjects and verbs agree. Also check to see whether semicolons and colons are used correctly.

A. Mark corrections and additions with proofreading marks from the box.

The students on the set-up team gathers at 815 in the morning. They arrange the soap, sponges, and hoses and then they put the signs out. The students on washing duty arrives at 900. They do the following things to each car soap it, scrub it, rinse it clean. The members of each crew rests for fifteen minutes however, no one at the site leave before 1200. This car wash will be fun, challenging, and rewarding.

B. Write the paragraph correctly on the lines below. Make the corrections and additions you marked above.

Name ______________________________

Sentences and Clauses

A **simple sentence** has one complete subject and one complete predicate.

Subject **Predicate**

Every culture has traditional stories and myths.

A **compound sentence** is made up of two or more simple sentences. Each simple sentence is called an *independent clause*. An **independent clause** has a subject and a predicate and can stand alone as a complete thought.

Independent Clause **Independent Clause**

Myths tell important things about the culture, and often the hero's traits are valued qualities in that culture.

A. Label each sentence **simple** or **compound.**

__________ **1.** For thousands of years, people have shared myths and legends; these myths make up one of humanity's great traditions.

__________ **2.** Many of these myths have come down to us.

__________ **3.** From Egypt, for example, comes the story of Osiris.

__________ **4.** In early Egyptian legends, Osiris was the god of vegetation, but in later myths, he was the ruler of the afterlife.

__________ **5.** Many of the most famous myths and legends come from Greece.

__________ **6.** The Greek myths and legends are thousands of years old, but people still enjoy reading them today.

B. Underline each independent clause in the sentences below.

7. Greek myths explain how nature works and why people act the way they do.

8. The people of Greece believed in many gods and goddesses, and they thought gods and goddesses dwelled in the underworld, the sea, land, and in the heavens.

9. Most of us know of Hercules; he was the strongest man in the world.

10. Hercules was given impossible tasks, but he was able to carry out every single one of them.

11. Many of these myths appear in *The Iliad* or *The Odyssey*; these famous poems come to us from Homer, the best-known poet of ancient Greece.

12. Much of what happens in those poems is myth, but archaeologists have used facts in the poems in their discovery of ancient Troy.

13. Myths and legends are more than interesting stories; they tell the history of a people.

Extension: Have students underline the independent clauses in the sentences in Part A.

Name

Complex Sentences

A **subordinate clause** has a subject and a predicate but cannot stand alone. It must be combined with an independent clause to express a complete thought.

Independent Clause / **Subordinate Clause**

Thanksgiving is a happy time when families across the nation gather together.

A complex sentence is a sentence that has an independent clause and a subordinate clause. In a complex sentence, the subordinate clause is introduced by a special conjunction called a **subordinating conjunction**.

Independent Clause / **Subordinate Clause**

Our family had a wonderful time when we visited the Robinsons on Thanksgiving.

Subordinating Conjunction (when)

Underline the subordinate clause in each sentence. Circle the subordinating conjunction.

1. Thanksgiving has been an American holiday since it began in the 1600s.
2. According to legend, the first Thanksgiving was in New England, at Plymouth, though this is not historically accurate.
3. When colonists arrived in Berkeley Plantation, Virginia, in 1619, their charter of rules called for a day of thanksgiving each year.
4. The first formal Thanksgiving did take place in Massachusetts, where Governor William Bradford proclaimed a day of thanksgiving for July 30, 1623.
5. Bradford wanted the holiday because the Massachusetts colony's fortunes changed for the better.
6. After colonists had suffered a winter of hardships, the first annual harvest was good.
7. While some colonists cooked, others hunted for fish, ducks, geese, and other game.
8. The colonists' Indian neighbors brought food, too, because their help had been crucial for the colonists' survival.
9. Everyone worked hard until the feast was finally ready.
10. Because that first feast was so meaningful, the custom of a thanksgiving day spread throughout the colonies.

Extension: Have students write five sentences containing a subordinate clause. Then have them underline the independent clause in each sentence.

Name ______________________________

Adjective Clauses

An **adjective clause** is a subordinate clause that modifies, or describes, a noun or pronoun in the independent clause of a complex sentence. An adjective clause usually begins with a **relative pronoun**, such as *who, whom, whose, which,* or *that*.

Relative Pronoun → that; **Adjective Clause** → that people of all ages enjoy

Story-telling is an activity that people of all ages enjoy.

Underline the adjective clauses.

1. Long ago, story-telling was one of the most important means of communication that people could have.
2. Stories were told by talented story-tellers, who viewed story-telling as an important art.
3. Everyone in the community listened to the stories, which played a key role in people's lives.
4. Many of the stories, for example, were ones that helped people understand their customs and traditions.
5. The story-tellers, whose tales were colorful and entertaining, often attracted large audiences.
6. The *Iliad* and *Odyssey* are classics that originally were told by a story-teller of ancient Greece.
7. The story of King Arthur and the Knights of the Round Table, which has fascinated people for hundreds of years, was passed down by these story-tellers.
8. The Grimm Brothers, who wrote down hundreds of fairy tales, collected these tales from traditional stories.
9. In America, folk tales and tall tales were stories that people enjoyed again and again.
10. The Native Americans, from whom many of our stories come, had a rich tradition of folk tales and myths.
11. Davy Crockett, Pecos Bill, and John Henry, who were the heroes of many of these stories, became legendary American heroes.
12. Today, books, films, and television, which are available almost everywhere, have taken the place of many story-tellers.
13. Many communities, however, have people who enjoy telling and hearing stories.
14. In many homes, parents tell stories that children love to hear night after night.

Extension: Have students draw an arrow from each of the adjective clauses in the sentences on this page to the noun or pronoun that it modifies.

Name

Adverb Clauses

An **adverb clause** is a subordinate clause that modifies the verb in the independent clause of a complex sentence. It tells **how, when, where, why,** or **under what condition** the action takes place. Adverb clauses usually begin with a **subordinating conjunction**, such as *because, when*, or *although*.

Subordinating Conjunction Adverb Clause

People all over the world love dance because of its movement.

Underline the adverb clauses.

1. As you know, people all over the world have their own dances.
2. Because of their special beauty, the dances of the Far East have gained enormous fame.
3. Although thousands of Chinese dances exist, all come from a few ancient dances.
4. These dances were performed when special needs or occasions arose.
5. In India, people "hear" stories when they see a dance.
6. Dance is very important in India because it has religious importance.
7. Because it is supposed to be a gift from the god Siva, dancing never is done only for entertainment.
8. A prayer is made as each dance is performed.
9. When the dancers move, they tell the stories of Hindu gods and heroes.
10. Although the audience enjoys the dances immensely, people always remember the messages of these dances.
11. People know many of the dances by heart because they see them so often.
12. The Nautch dance, for example, is performed whenever an important festival or religious event is held.
13. Indian dances spread to other parts of the Far East when the people of India traveled.
14. As you can see from photographs and films, the traditional dances of many of these countries resemble Indian dances.
15. The dances became different, however, because each country had its own customs and beliefs.

Extension: Have students draw an arrow from each of the adverb clauses in the sentences on this page to the verb that it modifies.

PRACTICE-88

Name

Participles and Participial Phrases

A **participle** is a verb form that can be the main verb in a verb phrase. **Present participles** are formed by adding *ing* to the verb. **Past participles** are usually formed by adding *ed* to the verb.

The guide was smiling.
She had guided many groups on this tour before.

A present or past participle can also be used as an adjective to modify a noun or pronoun.

The smiling guide showed us into the auditorium.
The guided tour was about to begin.

A **participial phrase** includes a participle used as an adjective, plus any other words that complete the participle's meaning.

Smiling at the boy, the guide answered his question.
Guided by the young woman, we visited all the exhibits.

Underline the participles in these sentences. Write **main verb** if the participle is used as the main verb in a verb phrase. Write **adjective** if the participle is used as an adjective.

1. The Navajo have earned fame for their many accomplishments. ____________
2. Navajo blankets are treasured works of art. ____________
3. Sand pictures are an honored tradition among the Navajo. ____________
4. These pictures usually are created for important ceremonies. ____________
5. The artists gather colored rocks and stones. ____________
6. Grinding stones reduce the rocks to tiny particles of sand. ____________
7. The artists then make bright, patterned pictures with the sand. ____________
8. The emerging pictures are beautiful. ____________
9. The pictures are destroyed at the end of the ceremonies. ____________
10. Today, Navajo artists still are making pictures in this age-old way. ____________
11. Today, Navajo women are still weaving traditional blankets. ____________
12. The women use very old but working looms. ____________
13. Museums have displayed hundreds of these blankets. ____________
14. The Navajo have developed their art for hundreds of years. ____________

Extension: Have students write four sentences containing participles. Then have students exchange papers, underline the participle, and write whether the participle is used as the main verb in a verb phrase or as an adjective.

Name ______________________ **PRACTICE-89**

Gerunds

A **gerund** is a verb form ending in **ing** that is used as a noun. It can function as a subject or as a direct object in a sentence.

Subject ↓ **Direct Object** ↓

Running has transformed exercising.

A **gerund phrase** is a group of words that includes a gerund along with other words that complete its meaning.

Gerund Phrase

Running in a marathon is a difficult task.

Write whether the underlined word in each sentence functions as a **main verb** in a verb phrase, a participle used as an **adjective**, or as a **gerund**.

1. ______________ People have been running in marathons for many years.
2. ______________ Runners must be in excellent shape for this punishing race.
3. ______________ Today, marathons are reviving an ancient tradition.
4. ______________ Around 500 B.C., the Persian army was invading Greece.
5. ______________ The Athenian army fought the approaching Persians at Marathon.
6. ______________ The Athenians made a running charge against their enemy.
7. ______________ The Athenian victory was stunning.
8. ______________ The Persian ships, though, still were threatening Athens.
9. ______________ Losing was still possible for the Athenians.
10. ______________ Warning Athens of the Persian threat was absolutely necessary.
11. ______________ Racing all the way to the city was the only solution.
12. ______________ Pheidippides, the Athenians' fastest racer, was already running.
13. ______________ Pheidippides had just finished running to Sparta and back.
14. ______________ The striding Athenian runner set out.
15. ______________ Reaching the city in the least possible time was vital.
16. ______________ Racing for twenty-five miles at full speed was a difficult task.
17. ______________ Dying at the city gates was Pheidippides' fate.

Extension: Have students use the following gerunds to create gerund phrases in their own sentences: *running, traveling, riding,* and *operating.*

Name ______________________________

Infinitives

An **infinitive** is a verb form that can be used as a noun. It is formed by using the word *to* with the base form of the verb. It may be used as the subject of the sentence or the direct object.

Subject — **Direct Object**

To fly a kite is great fun. Stacey wants to learn.

An **infinitive phrase** is a group of words that includes an infinitive along with other words that complete its meaning.

To sail a kite through the air is fun.

Always be careful not to confuse an infinitive or infinitive phrase with a prepositional phrase that begins with *to.*

Infinitive — **Prepositional Phrase**

Stacey has begun to learn. She went to the park an hour ago.

Write whether the underlined words in each sentence are an **infinitive**, an **infinitive phrase**, or a **prepositional phrase**.

1. ______________________ Most of us have tried to fly a kite.
2. ______________________ We went to the park yesterday afternoon.
3. ______________________ To get the kite up was easy.
4. ______________________ To fly, the kite needed more breeze.
5. ______________________ The kite slowly floated to the ground.
6. ______________________ In China, people began to fly kites thousands of years ago.
7. ______________________ To frighten their enemies was the purpose of the kites.
8. ______________________ Whistling bamboo pipes were attached to the kites.
9. ______________________ To whistle, these bamboo pipes caught the wind.
10. ______________________ In science, kites also have been used to experiment.
11. ______________________ To study electricity was the reason for Benjamin Franklin's interest in kites.
12. ______________________ The Wright Brothers flew kites to learn about airplane flight.

Extension: Have students write sentences using the following infinitives as subjects: *to study, to investigate,* and *to write.*

Name

Mechanics: Using Commas with Clauses

Remember the following rules for using commas when writing sentences with clauses.

- Use a comma before the **conjunctions** *and*, *but*, and *or* in a compound sentence.

  Helen Keller lived a remarkable life, and she inspired millions.

- Use commas to set off an **adjective clause** that gives information that is not essential to the meaning of the sentence.

  Helen, who worked with her teacher, slowly mastered language and other skills.

- Use a comma after an **adverb clause** that begins a sentence.

  When she was left blind and deaf at the age of two, she spent several years as an unruly, uneducated child.

Add commas where they are needed in these sentences. Circle the number of any sentence that is correct and needs no commas.

1. Once she understood the purpose Helen Keller made rapid progress.
2. Spelling out letters and words with finger movements young Keller communicated with her teacher.
3. After she mastered sign language at the age of ten Keller decided to learn speech.
4. Keller took lessons from a teacher of the deaf, and she soon began to speak.
5. The task was difficult but soon Keller was enrolled in a college preparatory school.
6. When she wanted to go to college Keller chose Radcliffe College.
7. When she graduated at the age of twenty-four Keller received many honors.
8. She campaigned actively for the blind and her work assisted millions of sightless people.
9. She appeared before government organizations and she wrote many books and articles.
10. When she worked with wounded soldiers, she helped many World War II veterans adjust to their injuries.
11. Much of Keller's progress was due to the work of her teacher and Anne Sullivan remained with Keller for many years.
12. Because she suffered vision problems from childhood Sullivan herself was virtually blind.
13. Although Keller was a difficult pupil at first Sullivan worked with her constantly.
14. Her patience and efforts were rewarded when the girl began to progress rapidly.
15. Sullivan who remained with Keller until she herself died helped her pupil in countless ways.

Extension: Have students write two sample sentences for each of the rules about using commas described on this page.

Name

Vocabulary Building: Suffixes

A **suffix** is a word part that is added to the end of a word. Adding a suffix often changes the meaning of the word or its part of speech.

Suffixes That Form Nouns:

an	one that is of	ist	one who works at, or adheres to
er, or	one who or that which	ment	act, condition, or result of
ian	one skilled in	ness	quality, state, condition
ion	act, state, or result of	tion	act, state, or result of
ism	act, practice, or process of		

Suffixes That Form Adjectives:

able, ible	able to	less	lacking, without
an, ian	of or belonging to	ly	like in nature
ful	full of, marked by	ward	moving or tending toward
ish	like, suggesting	y	showing, suggesting

Underline the suffix in each word. Then use the suffix and root word to figure out its meaning. Write the meaning on the line.

1. creator ______________________
2. wishful ______________________
3. openness ______________________
4. westward ______________________
5. fearless ______________________
6. journalist ______________________
7. government ______________________
8. snobbish ______________________
9. dirty ______________________
10. remarkable ______________________
11. kingly ______________________
12. San Franciscan ______________________
13. realism ______________________
14. admission ______________________

Extension: Have students write five words containing five different suffixes listed on this page and then define each word. Have them check their definitions in the dictionary.

Name

PRACTICE-93

Grammar and Writing Connection: Parallel Structure

Parallel structure is a style of writing in which similar parts of a sentence are expressed with the same part of speech. You can use parallel structure to add style and clarity to your writing.

Not Parallel: Constellations are shaped like people, animals, and even look like familiar objects.

Parallel: Constellations are shaped like people, animals, and even familiar objects.

Parallel structure applies to nouns, verbs, adjectives, and adverbs.

Rewrite each sentence so that it has parallel structure.

1. People have studied the constellations for centuries and also have made up stories about the constellations.

2. The ancient Greeks believed that constellations could control people's lives as well as making the weather.

3. The position of the Pole Star never changes and always to point due north.

4. Constellations were studied by the ancient Greeks, Chinese, Babylonians, and people living in Egypt.

5. Ancient astronomers observed the stars, noted their movements in the heavens, and were organizing the stars into patterns, or constellations.

Extension: Have students write four sentences that are not parallel. Then have students exchange papers and rewrite the sentences so that they have parallel structure.

Name ______________________________

Group Writing: A Research Report

A **research report** gives factual information about a topic. The information is gathered from library resources such as encyclopedias and other research books. When writing a research report, you must find the information and take notes on it. Then, you make an outline based on the notes. Finally, you write the report, using the outline as a guide.

A research report should have at least three paragraphs including these three elements:
- an **introduction** that gives the topic sentence, or what the report will be about
- a **body** that contains facts and information about the topic you have learned from your research
- a **conclusion** that sums up or restates the information

Read this research report and then answer the questions that follow.

The discovery of the ruins of the ancient city of Pompeii (pom pā′) startled many people during the 1700s. The city, which was a favorite vacation spot of wealthy Romans, was completely destroyed in the year 79. The ancient Pompeiians had built their city in the shadow of a volcano, Mount Vesuvius (vi sü′ vē əs). Despite occasional rumblings from the volcano, the city prospered. Then, in A.D. 79, lava suddenly burst from the mouth of the volcano. In moments, the entire city of Pompeii was buried under almost fifteen feet of lava, ashes, and cinder.

The city lay undisturbed for centuries. Then, in 1748, a man digging in a vineyard discovered a buried wall. Soon, great excavations were under way in the area of what is now the city of Naples. Those excavations have continued right into the present, so that more than half of the ancient city has been uncovered.

Because of the speed with which the city was covered with volcanic material, much of Pompeii has been well preserved. In fact, visitors to the ancient city can stand in ancient courtyards and see very clearly what life in this city was like two thousand years ago. Few other places in the world give people such a real sense of life in the ancient world.

1. What is the topic of this report? ______________________________

2. What is the purpose of the report? ______________________________

3. What does the writer tell you in the first sentence? ______________________________

____

4. Where do you think the writer got the information for the report? ______________________________

____

5. What does the last paragraph tell the reader? ______________________________

____

Extension: Have students list the important steps in writing a research report.

PRACTICE-95

Name

Thinking and Writing: Understanding Cause and Effect

A **cause** is the reason why something happened, while an **effect** is what happened as a result of the cause. Making causes and effects clear to your readers can help them understand the subject of a research report better.

Underline the sentence or sentences that answer each question.

1. Doug is writing a report on the effects of diet on health. He wants to show some causes and effects of good health and diet. Which of the following pieces of information should he use?

a. In certain parts of Central Asia, people live for an average of 90 to 100 years.

b. Many healthful foods taste good.

c. Children often do not like healthful food.

d. People who primarily eat foods high in unsaturated fats have a higher rate of heart attacks than people who eat foods low in these fats.

e. Long-lived people in Central Asia eat a diet that is high in fiber and low in meat and other fatty foods.

f. Doug's mother works as a dietician at a local hospital.

g. Today, many people are concerned about their health and diet.

2. Kiko is reporting on some of the world's deadliest diseases. She wants to discuss how medical researchers have discovered the causes of several of these diseases. Which pieces of information should she use?

a. During the 1300s, bubonic plague killed almost 25% of the population of Europe.

b. Influenza has symptoms much like those of a common cold.

c. During World War II, almost 40% of the soldiers in hospitals were there because of malaria.

d. Malaria still must be guarded against today.

e. The fleas carried by rats infected people with the plague during the 1300s.

f. Thousands of people fled their homes to avoid the plague.

g. DDT and other mosquito-killing chemicals helped control the insects that carried malaria.

h. For centuries, people feared a return of the "Black Death," as they called bubonic plague.

i. Influenza took the lives of over 400,000 Americans shortly after World War I.

j. Malaria is spread by certain flies and mosquitoes.

Extension: Have students work in pairs to write sentences based on cause-and-effect relationships.

Name

Proofreading: Step 4

Indent	¶
Add	∧
Add a comma	∧,
Add quotation marks	∨ ∨
Add a period	⊙
Take out	ℓ
Capitalize	≡
Make a small letter	/
Reverse the order	∽

Read this paragraph about old Pueblo homes. Make sure that participial phrases are placed correctly. Also, make sure that commas are used correctly with adjective and adverb clauses.

A. Use proofreading marks from the box to mark changes and corrections in the paragraph.

Pueblo is a Spanish word that means "town or village." Old Pueblo homes shone in the sun built of dried bricks. Each Pueblo village consisted of separate homes in a row joined together. The buildings which had one or two stories, had only a few windows, that were set high off the ground. Enclosed by thick walls the Pueblo inhabitants were protected from the sun's rays as well as from other dangers blazing down from above.

B. Use the changes and corrections you marked above to write the paragraph correctly on the lines below.